False Accusations
Of Rape:

Lynching in the
21st Century

John Davis, B.A., J.D., LL.M.

False Accusations of Rape:

Lynching in the 21st Century

John Davis, B.A., J.D., LL.M.

DEDICATION

This book is dedicated to all of those who care for, and assist, the victims of false accusations of rape, or sexual assault, by predatory women, especially the 10,000 or more men "lynched" during the Jim Crow era without due process of law.

TABLE OF CONTENTS

ACKNOWLEDGMENTS

The Author and Publisher would like to thank Jane for all of her help and support, and without whose help this book would not have been possible.

FALSE ACCUSATIONS OF RAPE: LYNCHING IN THE 21ST CENTURY

By: John Davis, B.A., J.D., LL.M.

FORWARD
Devolution

As I write this, we are encountering in the mainstream media more and more examples of murder and torture of men falsely accused of rape.

The accounts in the news mimic those that are in the shameful past of the U.S., during the "Jim Crow"[1] era. During this shameful 100 year period, from approximately 1867 to 1965, over

---

[1] The name "Jim Crow" refers to one of the founders of the Ku

ten thousand men were lynched in the United States with no recourse to due process or equal protection of the laws.

The majority of the men tortured and lynched were accused of rape, and, many (perhaps most of them) were falsely accused of rape. We cannot know if the accusations of rape against them were true, or false, as in most cases they were denied the right to a trial (or a fair trial). The false accusations arose from a combination of hatred of men, a mass conception of men as disposable, a vile notion that women should be always be believed when they accuse men of rape, and a level of savagery and evil that history rarely documents.

Vastly multiplied by fear, and ignorance, these same factors are, in modern day, being applied to men in general, and, to the unfortunate men in our world who become the victims of false accusations of rape.

Rape is a serious crime. Rape is not as serious as murder, or torture, or dismemberment, or burning someone alive. Rape is not a crime that should, in any way, permit humans to regress to the point that is below the animals. Those who falsely accuse men of rape, or, attempt to lessen the due process to which men accused of rape are entitled, are more vile and loathsome than any rapist. To pretend otherwise is merely to license the most savage and regressive aspects of "humanity."

John Davis

Fontveille, March 2015

"False accusations of rape are not about sex . . . . like the crime of rape itself, false accusations of rape are about power." John Davis, B.A., J.D., LL.M.

PROLOGUE
"Man's inhumanity to man makes countless thousands morn."[2]

Rape has become an obsession with the mainstream media throughout the world. The obsession has little to do with raising consciousness, accomplishing social justice, or enlightening people of the world. The mainstream media's obsession with rape has everything to do with making excuses for totalitarian government actions, raising the profits of media car-

---

[2] From Robert Burns' *"Man was made to Mourn: A Dirge,"* 1785.

tels, and advancing a hatred of men that is convenient for social and political institutions.

Figure 1 - A lynching in March of 2015 in Nagaland, India. Crowds, led by young women in uniform, broke into a high security prison and kidnapped a man accused of rape. The man was beaten to death with bamboo poles. This photo was taken hours before the medical examiner announced that there had been no rape, and the accusations by a 19 year-old accuser were false.

The media's obsession with rape has, intentionally, instilled a lynch mob mentality in the world's populace. This lynch mob mentality is directed solely at men, solely because it is convenient for the power base of gynocentric groups, and solely as a means of inciting sexual violence against men that is unequalled in history.

In more narrow circumstances, the bloodlust of lynch mobs, directed at men accused of rape, frequently hide racism, fascism, misandry, women's supremacy, or other perversions, as a motive to kill someone because of their creed, color, national origin or simply because they are men.

Mob violence is nothing new in the history of "(in)humanity."

The Salem witch hunts, the wholesale slaughter of Catholics in Elizabethan England, innumerable massacres as war crimes, the use of rape (by both men and women) to punish enemies, genocide (through violence or starvation), and countless mass "human" behaviors that are cruel beyond description, are all based upon one human perception – all of them are based upon the demonization of the victims.

The women of the Ku Klux Klan, for instance, had a long standing history of rape of African-

American Men. White women who raped African-American men is well-documented in nineteenth century literature.[3] This mass rape of African-American men, by privileged white women, is usually the subject of much revisionist history since the advent of second wave feminism. Modern feminism cloaks white women, who raped African-American men, as victims of "patriarchal" regulation of women's sexuality in the nineteenth century. The justification for white women to rape African-American men comes, in the mind of revisionist feminists, as a consequence of Southern women (having been "denied" their sexuality by the "Patriarchy") being "lonely and sad."[4] An incessant reference to a

---

[3] Fox-Genovese, Elizabeth. *Within the Plantation Household: Black and White Women of the Old South,* Chapel-Hill: University of North Carolina Press, 1988.

[4] For a pathetic apologist and revisionist view of white women who raped male slaves in the South, *see,* Jacqueline M. Allain, "*Sexual Relations Between Elite White Women and Enslaved Men in the Antebellum South: A Socio-Historical Analysis,*" 5 Student Pulse 08, pp. 2/3 (2013).
http://www.studentpulse.com/articles/747/2/sexual-relations-between-elite-white-women-and-enslaved-men-in-the-antebellum-south-a-socio-historical-analysis

fictional "patriarchy serves to demonize men, especially vulnerable men such as male African-American slaves, and gynocentric interests routinely use the patriarchy fiction to justify that demonization.

The fact is that privileged white women in the South, during the Jim Crow era, endangered millions of African-American men by raping them.

If a white woman raped a man in the *Ante-Bellum* (after the civil war) South, and it became known in a community, the woman would immediately accuse the African-American man of having forcibly raped her. This would trigger the lynch mobs and bloodlust of the community, to insure that the (innocent) African-American would be convicted (in the few cases in which there was a trial), but, more often simply tortured and murdered to cover up the fact that a white woman had raped him.[5]

---

[5] *Also see*, Apel, Dora, *Imagery of Lynching: Black Men, White Women, and the Mob*, Rutgers University Press

Whipping, beating, and other forms of torture were sometimes initiated before the actual hanging took place.

The lynching of Frank Embree   Missouri 1899

Figure 2 - The lynching of Frank Embree. Mr. Embree was never permitted a trial. He was tortured instead, mercilessly, until he finally confessed. He was then castrated and hung. No evidence has ever been presented of his guilt.

Mob violence, or "lynching" has been a problem throughout history, however, with the advent of Twentieth Century technology, a new dimension appeared in the miasma surrounding lynching – that new factor is the power of mass media.

Early in the twentieth century, many people began to understand the power of mass media. Whereas newspapers were often constrained in distribution to the geographic areas in which they were printed, the international reach of radio created a new means of influencing the minds of hundreds of millions of people.

Early in the history of radio, Orson Welles proved the power of mass media to create hysteria in millions of people.

On Halloween, 1938, Welles, a talented radio producer and director, created a sensation that would go down in history not just as a hoax, but as proof of the ability to manipulate tens of millions of people into believing something that has no basis in reality.

Welles constructed a play, based upon the science fiction novel "The War of the Worlds." The War of the Worlds involved a scenario in the nineteenth century in which the inhabitants of Mars, a race of alien beings, invades the Earth by arriving in extra-terrestrial vehicles.

The program was designed to allow the radio audience to believe they were listening to a news program. Orson Welles, (not to be confused with the author of the science fiction book who was named: "H.G. Wells"), had written a brilliant script that made it appear, to listeners, that the normal programming for the radio station was being interrupted by news flashes.

The result was that millions of listeners believed that an actual invasion from the planet Mars was underway.

The listeners who believed that the broadcast was real, literally disregarded any and all logical clues that the broadcast was merely fictional. They disregarded, for instance, that the broadcast reported massive troop mobilizations, and, international conventions of governing bodies, occurring in a time span that was less than the 40 minutes of the program.

The "War of the Worlds" broadcast of 1938

underscores the power of mass media to delude people, against all facts and logic, to believe something that is not even remotely grounded in reality. This power of mass media delusion is what is at the basis of all lynch mob mentality.

During the first part of the twentieth century in the U.S., a mass movement was in place that would ultimately take advantage of mass media, and mob mentality, to justify the lynching of over 10,000 men based on false (or unproven) accusations of rape. This period in U. S. history is often understated because it is an international and humanitarian disgrace.

That period is known as "the Jim Crow Era." During this era, the American Ku Klux Klan (See Chapter 3) had a virtual stranglehold on the workings, attitudes and laws of much of U.S. Government on both the federal and local levels. Though often misconceived as a small and radical movement in the U.S., at its peak in 1925, large segments of the U.S. population, in both the North and the South, were active members in the Ku Klux Klan. Scholars estimate, for example, that at the turn of the century, there were 5,000,000 women who belonged to the KKK.[6] One scholar has shown that fully twenty five percent of [white] women in the state of Indiana were members of the Ku Klux Klan.[7]

In the U.S., the KKK succeeded is establishing, in governments, the education system, and in the developing mass media certain Klan values: (a) that women were superior to men, and (b) that men were disposable in the service of women.

The U. S. Government was eventually able to shut down the KKK, and force it underground, by prosecuting it for tax evasion. The final knell of the organized Klan occurred in the 1960's when the Catholic President John F. Kennedy focused federal resources on eliminating racial prejudice against African-Americans in the U.S.

----

[6] This was roughly 14% of the women in the United States (based on U.S. Census data).

[7] Hill, Jackie (2008) "*Progressive Values in the Women's Ku Klux Klan,*" *Constructing the Past*: Vol. 9: Iss. 1, Article 6. Available at: http://digitalcommons.iwu.edu/constructing/vol9/iss1/6

However, the misandrist values of the Klan perpetuated themselves in various federal, state and local governments, and, eventually surfaced during the late 1960's as the second wave of feminism. Second wave feminism arose, not coincidentally, to take up the role of prosecuting misandry in the U.S., and abroad, when the KKK was no longer able to function because of government oversight.

The rise, reign and demise of the KKK coincided with yet another "lynch mob" in Europe that was very much parallel to the KKK lynch mobs in the U.S.

At the same time as the "War of the Worlds," and the peak of KKK power in the U.S., National Socialism in Germany, had been using the exact same propaganda techniques, for two decades, to set the stage for repeated mob violence in Europe.

In his extraordinary book, *"Brave New World Revisited,"*[8] Aldous Huxley wrote about the Nazi

---

[8] Huxley, Aldous, "Brave New World Revisited," First Edition, Harper (1958). It is helpful to read only the first edition of this book. In subsequent editions, post-war revisionists significantly omitted key sections of Huxley's brilliant work in order to

use of propaganda in WWII. He pointed out that the German people would not have been so deluded by a mad person, like Hitler, except for certain reasons. One of those reasons was Hitler's command over the mass media to spread propaganda.

Through that campaign of propaganda, often connected with a sexual context for additional emotional hysteria, Hitler was able to turn tens of millions of people against Jews, Americans, Slavs, and many other people in the world. It was this propaganda that fueled hatred that drove the German people, mostly unconscious that they were being driven, to cooperate with the National Socialists in institutionalizing hatred against certain groups of people, and engage in genocide on an unprecedented scale.

As Huxley pointed out, a reading of Hitler's "Mein Kampf" shows that he was a deluded and paranoid person. However, there is one section of "Mein Kampf" in which Hitler is very clear in his understanding and in which he demon-

---

make it more "politically correct" and palatable to post-war readers.

strates genius. That section of "Mein Kampf" is Hitler's dissertation on the use of mainstream (mass) media to spread propaganda. This section of "Mein Kampf" became the blueprint for Madison Avenue advertising firms, as well as the political campaigns in the U.S. after WWII, and, in the rest of the world.

Although the usefulness of propaganda has been demonstrated by warmongers and politicians, throughout history, beginning in the ancient world, the use of modern mass media (especially television and radio) in the twentieth century saw refinements to propaganda techniques. These propaganda techniques are now common in the mainstream media across the world. They have been adopted in the U.S., by feminism and political entities supporting feminism, so that the feminist propaganda techniques are indistinguishable from the techniques employed by the Nazis during WWII.

Let's examine some of that Nazi propaganda, and compare it to the feminist propaganda that exists in the current U.S. climate of rape hysteria.

Der Nürnberger Jude Otto Mayer

pflegte seine Opfer zu kreuzigen. In völlig nacktem Zustande band
er sie an ein eigens dazu angefertigtes Holzkreuz und schändete
sie, sobald aus den Wundmalen das Blut floß.

Figure 8h. A Nazi cartoon. The caption reads: "Otto Mayer,
the Nuremberg Jew, used to crucify his victim. He bound her,
stark naked, to a specially prepared wooden cross, and raped
her as soon as the blood began to flow from her wounds."

This propaganda piece shows the elements of
mainstream media generating hatred, hysteria
and justifications for violence against Jews. The
same elements are evident in feminist and gynocentric propaganda in the Twenty First century.

The components of this cartoon involve, first,

the identification of the enemy. In this case, the enemy is identified as a group of people (Jewish men) whom the Nazis wanted the populace to hate. That hate was useful to the Nazis as it enabled them to seize the assets of Jewish interests in Germany, after WWI, and assist the Nazi's in rebuilding Germany. (In modern day feminist propaganda, it is usually not necessary to identify men as the target of the propaganda).

The second component of the cartoon is to introduce a nubile woman (the universal symbol of "innocence," purity and desirability) as a "victim" of the target class of hate and deception (the Jewish men). The cartoon emphasizes the sexual appeal of the woman for a very good reason. As Madison Avenue advertisers learned shortly after WWII – "sex sells." What could be a greater motivator to young German men, very vulnerable, under the heavy influence of youthful hormones, to mindlessly join the Nazi campaign to demonize and eradicate Jews? Indeed, the U.S., itself, used the same propaganda on young U.S. men to encourage them to enlist as "cannon fodder" in WWI.

Demonization of the target class is the third objective of this particular propaganda piece. The man is portrayed as ugly, sadistic, barbaric, without conscience and in the mindless pursuit of sexual self-gratification. It is identical to the modern feminist propaganda which seeks to establish that "all men are rapists" and that all men would rape uncontrollably if the class of people, known as men, were not constrained by draconian laws effectively presuming that they are sexual criminals.

"All men are rapists and that's all that they are." – Marilyn French

MEN SERVE A MUCH HIGHER PURPOSE THAN JUST YOUR FANTASIES, MARILYN

In modern day mass media, gynocentric and feminist groups are, literally, advocating the presumption that a man is a rapist unless he can prove his innocence.

This is evident in American law in what are

known as "rape shield" statutes. Ostensibly, "rape shield" statutes were designed to protect victims from harassment. What they have done, in reality, however, is protect false rape accusers from the consequences of their false accusations of rape. They have also served to accelerate the convictions of innocent men.

A few gynocentric jurisdictions have ruled that a trial judge has the discretion, under rape shield statutes, to exclude evidence of the accuser's prior history of making false accusations of rape.[9] A woman's purely sexual history, as all

---

[9] Initially, the admissibility of false accusations of rape were admissible to question the credibility of an accuser. *Commonwealth v. Bohannon*, 376 Mass. 90, 378 N.E.2d 987 (1978).

In *Bohannon*, the Massachusetts Supreme Judicial Court held that evidence of prior false rape allegations was admissible to impeach the complaining witness's credibility. The use of such evidence did not implicate the state's "rape-shield" statute because it "dealt with prior allegations of rape; [it] in no way sought to elicit a response concerning the complainant's prior sexual activity or reputation for chastity."

The *Bohannon* court disclaimed any special rule regarding the credibility of women in rape cases. Rather, the court approached the issue of prior false claims generally, pointing out that prior false accusations of the specific crime that is the subject of the trial might seriously damage the complainant's

legal scholars agree, is not relevant to the issue of whether she has consented, on any given occasion, to sex. Consequently, evidence that a woman has had a history of promiscuity, prostitution, or even sexual relations with the accused, is not admissible to show that the woman consented to sex on a particular occasion.

Nevertheless, evidence that a woman having made prior false accusations of rape is directly, and should be directly, admissible to attack her credibility in a trial in which her consent is the determining issue as to whether a rape occurred.

One Wisconsin trial judge, however, to insure that a man was convicted of rape, ruled that evidence a victim had previously lied about the use of force, in another rape she had claimed, was inadmissible to cast doubts on the credibility of the victim in a subsequent case.

The trial judge invoked a legal fiction for her ruling in that case. A woman claimed that a

---

credibility. Because of the special dangers in these cases, however, an offer of proof that indicates a strong factual basis for the questions is required.

man had forcibly raped her. She had made the same claim in another case years earlier when she was 13 and the (statutory) rapist was 21 years old. Initially, she had claimed that the 21 year old man had forcibly raped her. She later retracted that false claim, and, the man was convicted solely of statutory rape (as opposed to the more serious crime of first degree rape by force.)

The fact that she had once lied about the use of force in having sex with another man, even though he was eventually convicted of only having sex with an underage person, is directly relevant as to whether she is lying the second time she accuses a man of forcible rape.

Nonetheless, the judge "reasoned" that since the first man had been convicted of statutory rape, without the use of force, there had been a sexual assault and that the woman's lie about the use of force should not be admissible in the trial against the second man she accused of using force.[10]

---

[10] *State v. Christopher Walter Hurns*, 2011AP857-CR, District 1, (Wisconsin, May 8, 2012). (Not recommended for pub-

The result of these perversions in the laws of evidence is that false accusations of rape very much operate as sexual violence against men.

These perversions of law are a direct result of the hatred that gynocentric propaganda instills and encourages in the legal system, the education system, and most other institutions in the U.S. and across the world.

Let's take a look at some of this propaganda.

lication).

Modern Madison avenue advertising (propaganda) techniques include some innovations to the obvious propaganda of the Nazi era.

Modern propaganda techniques rely upon insinuations and innuendo, rather than direct demonization, to assault the target class. For instance, in Figure 3 above, a man is not shown in the photograph. However, the propaganda slogan "real men do not rape" leaves no doubt as to the intended innuendo that "all men are rapists" (and women are merely victims). The insinuation is that all men are inherently evil rapists, and, that our culture must take violent action, in the form of suspending due process, to insure that women have a special protected status in any situation in which a man and a woman have sex.

Let's examine another piece of propaganda that shows a man, and, makes it clear that men are the direct target of the hatred and demonization of the propaganda.

Figure 4 - A misandrist meme that places the onus of preventing rape solely upon men. This type of political propaganda uses innuendo and insinuations to demonize men as rapists.

In this piece of propaganda, the insinuation is that the "man next door" is a rapist, simply because he is a man, and, that he should control his inherently evil predisposition to rape women indiscriminately.

Modern research shows that women rape men more often than men rape women. Instead of using force, women typically use alcohol, drugs, deceit, threats (including threats of falsely accusing male victims of rape) in order to rape men.[11] Yet the foregoing propaganda seeks to establish only men as rapists, and, women only as "victims" who must be protected at all costs to the disposable men who will surely rape them if drastic measures are not implemented.

That special protected status, that feminists and gynocentric political interests are seeking, includes the right to falsely accuse a man, with impunity. This was exactly the power that women had during the "Jim Crow" era in the U.S., when a woman's accusation of rape was not required to withstand the test of due process. The result of that method, which modern feminism is seeking through its propaganda, was evident to the entire world.

The modern feminist propaganda sets the stage for women in modern culture using false accusations of rape as a means of committing sexual violence against men.

------

[11] This is covered exhaustively in the author's books: Women Who Rape Men, and, Female Sex Predators: A Crime Epidemic (available on Amazon).

Figure 5 - Burned alive based solely upon an unproven accusation of rape by a white woman.

Modern feminism, and their allied interests in politics, literally seek a return to the days in which men will not have the benefit of due process if accused of rape.

Figure 6 - Hung, castrated and burned alive based solely upon the accusation or rape of a white woman. The lynching of Jesse Washington was far from an isolated occurrence in the U.S. Modern feminist groups seek to engender hatred toward men, as a gender, to justify similar atrocities at some time in the future.

For decades, this power of the media, has been utilized by the worldwide media to delude the public into believing that there is a "rape epidemic" in the United States and the rest of the world.

Man-hating propaganda in the U.S. is not just limited to posters, television programs and social media memes. It extends across the entire fabric of the information, legal and education systems in the U.S. and around the world. The result is "rape hysteria" that drives sexual violence against men, rooted in false accusations of rape or sexual misconduct against men, and men alone.

CHAPTER 1
Rape Hysteria

LYING WITH RAPE STATISTICS – RAPE STATISTIC PROPAGANDA

Of all the statistics available in the information age, rape statistics are the most elusive.

Statistics on rape are inherently unreliable because of the political, and gynocentric,[12] interests that stand to gain from exaggerating the amount of rape that occurs.

------

[12] *Gynocentric*, Syllabification: gy·no·cen·tric ADJECTIVE: Centered on or concerned exclusively with women; taking a female (or specifically a feminist) point of view. Oxford English Dictionary (2014).

Rape is considered such a serious crime, that a mere accusation of rape is sufficient to ruin an accused. Consequently, the power to falsely accuse of rape is a coveted power. It enables someone to invoke massive law enforcement resources, based upon a mere accusation, and, it empowers someone to inflict immense injury on a falsely accused without having to comply with due process. (Even though a majority of rape accusations are proven to be false, the mere accusation, or arrest, of an innocent person on rape charges is sufficient to make that person unemployable, and, a semi-permanent subject of hatred and scorn in any community).

The result is that gynocentric interests ridiculously exaggerate the number of actual rapes that occur.

This exaggeration of the incidence of rape in the U.S. reached hysterical proportions in 2013 and 2014, and, eventually the mainstream media began to question the hysteria.[13]

---

[13] *See, e.g.*, Will, George, "*Colleges become the victims of progressivism*," Washington Post (June 6, 2014). http://www.washingtonpost.com/opinions/george-quewill-college-become-the-victims-of-

Once a major mainstream commentator began to apply logic, reason and verifiable statistics to the rape propaganda and hysteria, the mainstream media response was shock, horror and disbelief. Rather than correct the exaggerated statistics, many mainstream media outlets simply engaged in massive denial.

In a typical response, to suppress accurate statistics, and analysis, of the rape hysteria in the U.S. media, many pundits called for the resignation of anyone who questioned that "1 in 5 women on college campuses are raped;" or that " 1 in 4 women will be raped in their lifetime;" or that "rape is an epidemic in our colleges and universities."

These falsified statistics, to make matters worse, usually originated from government sources. Since they originated from government sources, many people mistakenly believed that "they must be true." In truth, the exaggerated statistics are the product of political corruption over those captive agencies.

---

progressivism/2014/06/06/e90e73b4-eb50-11e3-9f5c-9075d5508f0a_story.html

How is it possible for government statistics to be so corrupted as to represent a fraud on the public?

To answer this question, one must look at the techniques used by those who profit from the "rape industry" in the U.S. The principal benefactors of rape hysteria are in government itself.

Politicians, by promoting rape hysteria, seek to generate votes for themselves by pretending to be "tough on crime" and "fighting the rape problem in the U.S." These politicians often gain enough votes from rape hysteria to make a difference in an election. Consequently, if one candidate promotes rape hysteria, and, promotes herself as a solution to rape hysteria, then, any other candidate in the election arena must do the same, or risk being labeled "misogynistic."

The second largest pool of benefactors from rape hysteria are the police and law enforcement lobbies. With the war on drugs de-escalating, police agencies need new job and funding justifications. Police agencies therefore promote rape hysteria in order to justify additional funding for their departments and staffing budgets.

The third largest pool of benefactors of rape hysteria are the government agencies, and NGO's, that depend on government funding for their rape programs, and programs related to sexual assault.

The final group which profits from the generated rape hysteria is the world-wide mainstream media. Through shocking headlines, the global mainstream media sells numerous stories and commentaries, each purporting to "expose" a "vast rape epidemic" (much like Senator McCarthy "exposed" purportedly rampant anti-American activities in the 1950's).[14]

U.N. RAPE HYSTERIA FRAUD

One example of media hysteria, and rape paranoia involves the United Nations claiming that 1 in 4 Asian men admit to having "raped" their intimate partner. In September of 2013, news outlets around the world, festooned international media feeds with the following head-

---

[14] Compare Senator Kirsten Gillibrand's (D-N.Y.) current "sexual assault crusade, with the anti-communist crusade of Senator Joseph McCarthy (R-Wis.) in the 1950's.

lines:

Almost a quarter of men 'admit to rape in parts of Asia'[15]

News outlet, after news outlet, spread these headlines across the globe. Not one of the journalists" commenting on this headline made any attempt to analyze the basis for the headline.

The basis for the headline was a United Nations study, done by the U.N. Commission on Women.

On the questionnaire purporting to expose "rape," out of twenty questions, one of the questions was:

> "Have you ever had sex with your partner when you knew she didn't want to but you thought she should agree because she's your wife/ partner?"

If the man answered this question in the affirmative, he was classified as a rapist. The

---

[15] Tulip Mazumdar, "Almost a quarter of men 'admit to rape in parts of Asia'," BBC News – Health, September 9, 2013. http://www.bbc.com/news/health-24021573

U.N.'s reasoning for classifying one fourth of the male participants as rapists was that they were rapists not because they forced their partner to have sex, but, because they "felt entitled" to sex with their partner even though she might not have wanted to have sex at the time.

There was no control survey done on women to determine how many women would answer the question in the affirmative. However, other studies strongly suggest that women also feel entitled to have sex with their husband or male partner, in a long-term relationship, even if their male partner is not fully "in the mood."[16]

Most rational people who have experienced healthy interpersonal relationships have, at one time or another, in those relationships, had sex with their partner even if they did not want to have sex. This is a normal part of compassion-

---

[16] Charlotte Alter, "*Nearly Half of Young Men Say They Have Had Unwanted Sex*," Time Magazine, March 25. 2014. http://time.com/37337/nearly-half-of-young-men-say-theyve-had-unwanted-sex/; French, B. H., Tilghman, J. D., & Malebranche, D. A. (2014, March 17). Sexual CoercionContext and Psychosocial Correlates Among Diverse Males. Psychology of Men &Masculinity. Advance online publication. http://dx.doi.org/10.1037/a0035915.

ately addressing needs of a partner in an intimate relationship. It is not "rape" except to those who are striving for excuses to raise rape hysteria and paranoia.[17]

COLLEGE CAMPUS RAPE HYSTERIA

As another example, in January of 2014, the White House undertook a one-sided campaign to protect women on college campuses from rape and sexual assault.[18] (The campaign openly placed all responsibility for sexual assault on men, and, men alone. The campaign made no effort to address the rate of sexual assault of men on campuses, which is higher than it is for women).

Note: A recent (2002) study commissioned by the National Institute of Mental Health, and

---

[17] *See*, Ruth Alexander, "How Many Men in Asia Admit to Rape?" BBC News Magazine, November 1, 2013. http://www.bbc.com/news/magazine-24713110

[18] Jackie Calms, "Obama Seeks to Raise Awareness of Rape on Campus," NEW YORK TIMES, January 22, 2014. http://www.nytimes.com/2014/01/23/us/politics/obama-to-create-task-force-on-campus-sexual-assaults.html?_r=0

conducted by the University of Illinois details the dynamics of women who rape men.[19]

>*Only recently have researchers begun to examine sexual coercion directed toward men [citations omitted] Struckman-Johnson (1988)[20] and Struckman-Johnson (1998)[21] found 43% of men sampled reported experiencing a coercive incident, of which 36% reported unwanted touch and 27% reported being coerced into sexual intercourse. Research examining both men and women as perpetrators and victims of coercive or aggressive behavior found that men and women experience comparable levels of physical violence in dating relationships (McConaghy & Zamir, 1995;[22] Sigelman, Berry, &*

---

[19] Debra L. Oswald, PhD, Brenda L. Russell, "*Sexual Coercion and Victimization of College Men*," 17 J. INTERPERSONAL VIOLENCE 3, pp. 273-285 (March 2002). (One hundred and seventy-three men were recruited from undergraduate courses at a private Midwestern University. Mean age of respondents was 20.94 (SD = 3.48). (n=173).

[20] Struckman-Johnson, C., "Forced sex on dates: It happens to men too." 24 JOURNAL OF SEX RESEARCH 234-241 (1988).

[21] Struckman-Johnson, C., & Struckman-Johnson, D. "The dynamics and impact of sexual coercion of men by women." In P. B. Anderson, & C. Struckman-Johnson (Eds.), "Sexually aggressive women: Current perspectives and controversies" (pp. 121-143). New York: Guilford.

[22] McConaghy, N., & Zamir, R., "Heterosexual and homosex-

Wiles, 1984)[23]. . . . . These studies reveal that victimization of men occurs with some regularity; . . . .[24]

These studies show that 27% of college men have been raped by women. (I.e., according to the new federal definitions of rape, the men have been subjected to coerced intercourse without their consent).[25]

In April of 2014, the White House Task Force purportedly assigned to preventing campus sexual assault, issued its first report.[26]

The White House made no effort to conceal

---

ual coercion, sexual orientation and sexual roles in medical students." 24 ARCHIVES OF SEXUAL BEHAVIOR, 489-502 (1995).

[23] Sigelman, C. K., Berry, C. J., & Wiles, K. A. "Violence in college students' dating relationships," 5 JOURNAL OF APPLIED SOCIAL PSYCHOLOGY, 530-548 (1984).

[24] Oswald & Russell, *supra* at 274.

[25] United States Department of Justice, *An Updated Definition of Rape*, http://blogs.justice.gov/main/archives/1801 January 6, 2012.

[26] "FACT SHEET: Not Alone – Protecting Students from Sexual Assault," White House Office of the Press Secretary, April 14, 2014 http://www.whitehouse.gov/the-press-office/2014/04/29/fact-sheet-not-alone-protecting-students-sexual-assault

its gynocentric, gender-specific campaign. Mainstream media bombarded the public with a fraudulent statistic that claimed 1 in 5 women would be sexually assaulted on college campuses in the U.S.

The White House "statistics," however, were literally a fantasy statistic. The statistic of 1 in 5 women in college being subjected to sexual assault was based entirely on what is known as "advocacy research."[27] ("Advocacy research" is "research" that is not really "research;" it is merely the product of persons who, without any objectivity or any adherence to the scientific method, searches for specious and spurious bits of data, often abstracted out of context, to support their own personal biases and prejudices.)[28]

To make matters worse, careless, or outright deceptive, advocacy journalism began confusing "sexual assault" with "forcible rape." With the

---

[27] Christina Hoff Sommers, "CDC study on sexual violence in the U.S overstates the problem," WASHINGTON POST, January 27, 2012. http://www.washingtonpost.com/opinions/cdc-study-on-sexual-violence-in-the-us-overstates-the-problem/2012/01/25/gIQAHRKPWQ_story.html

[28] Id.

typical accuracy of zealots, the mainstream media began disseminating headlines that stated: 1 in 5 women on college campuses will be raped while attending colleges and universities in the U.S.

The fact is, that according to FBI statistics, in all of the College Campuses and Universities in the U.S., combined, there were only 485 forcible rapes known in a typical college year.

1 in 5 women raped on College Campuses?

F.B.I Stats Confirm that in 2010 There were a TOTAL of 485 known rapes on all U. S. College Campuses COMBINED

[Source: FBI Statistics on Offenses Known to Law Enforcement by State by University and College 2010]

End Rape Hysteria

THE EFFECTS OF RAPE HYSTERIA?

The effects of Rape Hysteria are almost never addressed by either the media or government agencies.

The first effect is that innocent men are frequently arrested on false rape charges.

False accusations of rape would fairly full a complete volume to properly explore. We can only summarize, in this report, the devastating effects on a man who is falsely accused of rape.

There are examples of falsely accused men who have been subjected to severe violence, permanent loss of employment, shunning in the community, and, more devastatingly, false imprisonment or death at the hands of lynch mobs.

We have only to look to our recent, barbaric past in the U.S., and in other countries, to know that men who are falsely accused often lose their lives (without any possibility of due process of law).

Figure 7 - Lynchings of Men falsely accused of rape were common under Jim Crow in the U.S.

Gynocentric political interests are quick to cite a fantasy statistic that only 2% of rape claims are false. However, the 2% figure has been proven to be a sham statistic that has no basis in reality. The 2% figure was a completely contrived figure invented by a novelist in the 1970's. As with most propaganda, it was repeated endlessly (and erroneously) until it became accepted as truth. That figure, of only 2% of rape claims being false, however, has been thoroughly debunked by legal scholars.[29]

The next most common statistic on false rape claims, advanced by gynocentric interests, is a figure that only 8% of rape complaints are false. This figure was taken from stock language in FBI reports that has appeared, for years, in those reports, without any statistical substantiation by the FBI.[30]

---

[29] Edward Greer, The Truth behind Legal Dominance Feminism's Two Percent False Rape Claim Figure, 33 Loy. L.A. L. Rev. 947 (2000). Available at: http://digitalcommons.lmu.edu/llr/vol33/iss3/3

[30] "Complaints of all Crime Index offenses made to law enforcement agencies which are found to be false or baseless can be "unfounded" and excluded from crime counts. A higher percentage of complaints of forcible rape are determined "unfounded," or found by investigation to be false, than for any other Index crime. While the average of "unfounded" rates for all Crime Index offenses was 2 percent in 1997, 8 percent of forcible rape complaints were "unfounded" for the same timeframe." FBI, Uniform Crime Reports for the United states 1997, p. 26. "Nationally, over half of the forcible rapes reported to law enforcement were cleared by arrest or exceptional means during 1997. At 55 percent for suburban counties and 52 percent for rural counties, county law enforcement clearance rates were slightly higher than the city law enforcement clearance rate at 50 percent. (See Table 25.)" *Id.* In other words, although 8% of rape accusations were definitively determined to be false beyond any doubt, approximately 50% of the remaining accusations of rape had no evidence on which

The FBI reports, however, if they are carefully read by a person trained as a prosecutor, show not that the rate of false claims of rape is limited to 8%. The FBI reports show that the incidence of false claims of rape are *at least* 8%. Gynocentric pundits jump to the conclusion that this means that *only* 8% of rape complaints are false.

What inexpert analysts overlook in, jumping to this conclusion, is that just because law enforcement has determined that 8% of rape complaints are definitely false, does not mean that the remaining 92% of rape complaints are true.

In examining the FBI reports, on which people rely for the claim that the rate of false accusations of rape is only 8%, amateur analysts overlook the fact that those same reports state that [only] fifty percent of the rape complaints are "cleared by arrest." What this means, in law enforcement parlance, is that there was insufficient evidence to arrest anyone in 50% of the cases.[31]

---

to make an arrest.

[31] *See generally*, James McNamara and Jennifer Lawrence,

As any experienced prosecutor knows, the threshold of evidence required to make an arrest is extremely low. The 1980's and 1990's was a time in which courts dramatically adopted "law and order" rhetoric to remove constitutional protections for due process of law, and, make it almost impossible for a judge to rule that an arrest was made without probable cause. In most cases, the U.S. Supreme Court has lowered the evidentiary threshold for an arrest to the point where there is no effective threshold. The police may arrest someone merely upon an accusation of a complainant, a mere suspicion, or, even upon an anonymous insinuation.[32]

If the police do not have sufficient evidence to make an arrest in 50% of rape cases, although the police may not have definitively determined

---

"False Allegations of Adult Crimes," FBI Law Enforcement Bulletin, September 2012. (There are a large number of alleged sex crimes that although do not fall into the category of having been determined as "false," nevertheless fall into the category of being unsupported, or, too speculative as to be considered legitimate claims to form a basis for arrest and prosecution).

[32] This is known as a "post-constitutional society." See generally, J. Andrew P. Napolitano, "Constitutional Chaos: What Happens When the Government Breaks Its Own Laws," 2006.

that those 50% of rape claims are false, it is reasonable to conclude that those 50% of rape claims, for which there is insufficient evidence to make an arrest, are also false claims.

Independent, mainstream studies, confirm this analysis of FBI statistics and reports on false allegations of rape.

The two most cited studies are also those that gynocentric interests most seek to suppress and conceal from the mainstream media.

A look at these sources, however, shows that the studies (although subjected to a barrage of negative rhetoric from feminist groups and those promoting rape hysteria) are sound. They are the only studies that were conducted according to scientific principles, and, remain un-refuted by any other similar studies.

The first study is known as the *"Kanin Study."*[33]

---

[33] Eugne Kanin, Ph.D., *False Rape Allegations*, ARCHIVES OF SEXUAL BEHAVIOR, VoL 23, No. L (1994).
http://blog.lib.umn.edu/jbs/maysession/KaninFalseRapeAllegations.pdf

The *Kanin Study* was conducted before "rape shield" statutes[34] effectively prohibited scientific and objective inquiries into actual rape cases.

The *Kanin Study* is actually in two parts. Dr. Kanin first analyzed rape cases at a Midwestern city's police department. About 41% of the women who had made complaints that they had been raped, on further investigation, admitted that their rape complaints were false. There was a sufficient number of participants to allow Kanin to infer that, in the general population of rape complaints, about 41% of rape claims are false (with a margin of error of about 7 points).

However, several years after the first study,

---

[34] A thorough discussion of "rape shield statutes," and how they impair scientific studies on the subject of false accusations of rape, is beyond the scope of this report. Briefly, rape shield statutes prohibit law enforcement, prosecutors and defense counsel from inquiring into the circumstances of a rape accusation, and details about the rape accuser. Rape shield statutes, effectively, require that law enforcement or prosecutors, and courts, minimize the efforts to question the validity of a rape claimant's allegations as to whether or not the allegation is true. There is little dispute among law enforcement personnel that rape shield statutes are responsible for many false accusations of rape, and, impair the integrity of investigations into claims of rape that are well-founded, as well as those that are spurious or false.

Kanin duplicated the experiment using campus police in Indianapolis (at Purdue University). The second study affirmed the first, and, showed that roughly 60% of rape complaints made to law enforcement were also false.

Dr. Kanin eventually concluded, through expert analysis, in a large population, nationwide, a report of rape was as likely to be false as it was to be true.

The second study, often suppressed as being "politically incorrect," and often assaulted by gynocentric interests, is a U. S. Air Force Study conducted by the U. S. Air Force Office of Special Investigations in 1984.[35] This study also pre-dates rape shield statutes and stands as one of the few scientifically based studies on the real rate of false accusations of rape. Like the *Kanin* study, gynocentric interests have viciously assaulted the study with rhetoric, and censored it,

---

[35] "False Allegations," FORENSIC SCIENCE DIGEST, V. 11, no. 4, Dec. 1985, p. 64, by Charles P. McDowell. The websites containing Col. McDowell's Air Force report are often "hacked" to keep people from accessing the report online. However, with some diligence, copies of the report may be found in various locations on the internet.

but there are no credible studies that contradict it.

This report, which was also based upon the unimpeachable admissions of the women making rape complaints that the allegations were false, fix the rate of false allegations of rape at about 65%.

A more recent report in the Forensic Examiner, by Dr. Bruce Gross, Ph.D., J.D., M.B.A., also confirms the actual rate of false accusations is somewhere between 50% and 60%.[36] Dr. Gross, in his paper, provides an extensive analysis of the phenomenon of false rape accusations in our current climate of rape hysteria in the U.S. (and abroad).

WHAT IS THE REAL RATE OF RAPE IN THE U.S.?

Our research for this work indicates that there are some reliable statistics available on the real incidence of rape. However, there are

---

[36] Bruce Gross, Ph.D., J.D., M.B.A, False Rape Allegations – An Assault on Justice, 2 FORENSIC EXAMINER (Spring 2009). http://www.theforensicexaminer.com/archive/spring09/15/

almost no reliable *analyses* of those rape statistics available.

The FBI has published an often suppressed statistic on the incidence of rape in the U.S. The FBI's statistic is that the incidence of rape is 26.9 rapes per 100,000 people in the U.S. Based upon a population estimate of 313,914,040 people in the United States, there were, in 2012, approximately 84,443 forcible rapes **reported** in the U.S. general population.

Although this is a "hard statistic," and would seem to indicate that there were 84,443 forcible rapes in the U.S. in 2012, it is important to realize that not all "reported rapes" constitute actual incidents of rape.[37]

In determining the actual rate of rape, in the U.S., one must take some factors into consideration and adjust the statistics.

---

[37] See *generally*, James McNamara and Jennifer Lawrence, *False Allegations of Adult Crimes*, FBI Law Enforcement Bulletin, September 2012. (There are a large number of alleged sex crimes that although do not fall into the category of having been determined as "false," nevertheless fall into the category of being unsupported, or, too speculative as to be considered legitimate claims to form a basis for arrest and prosecution).

The first factor is the amount of false rape reports. Our research conclusively established that roughly 60% of "reported rapes" are false. (See discussion, *supra,* and notes accompanying).

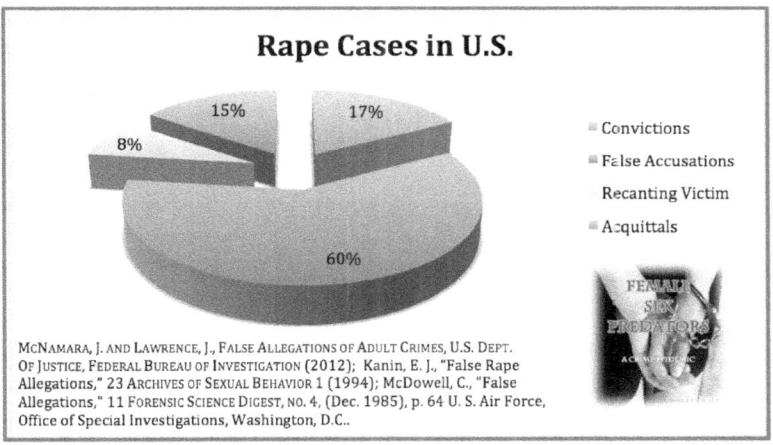

Rape Cases in U.S.

15%   17%

8%

60%

Convictions
False Accusations
Recanting Victim
Acquittals

McNamara, J. and Lawrence, J., False Allegations of Adult Crimes, U.S. Dept. Of Justice, Federal Bureau of Investigation (2012); Kanin, E. J., "False Rape Allegations," 23 Archives of Sexual Behavior 1 (1994); McDowell, C., "False Allegations," 11 Forensic Science Digest, no. 4, (Dec. 1985), p. 64 U. S. Air Force, Office of Special Investigations, Washington, D.C..

About half of the rapes that are taken to trial result in acquittals, and another 8% of "reported rapes" result in exonerations (with the accuser recanting the accusation of rape, or DNA evidence exonerating the accused).

The chart above shows the statistical adjustments that must be made to the number of "reported rapes" in order to arrive at an accurate number of actual forcible rapes.

Realistically, only 17% of "reported rape" cases are actual cases of rape. This would seem to indicate that the actual number of rapes occurring in the U.S. in 2012 was 14,355 rapes. That figure yields an adjusted statistical probability of a woman being raped, in a given year, at one in 11,371. (We would emphasize that even one case of forcible rape is abhorrent in any culture. However, we would also emphasize that the rate at which men are raped by women, likely exceeds the rate at which men rape women. Consequently, we believe that statistics must begin to reflect the actual rate of rape that includes the incidents of women who rape men. This is the subject of another of our studies).[38]

However, to arrive at an accurate figure of rape, one must make another major adjustment.

The FBI statistics do NOT include the numbers of women who rape men in which men are the victims and women are the offenders. The numbers of women who rape men have been intentionally excluded from federal statistics up

---

[38] Davis, John, BA., J.D., LI.M., "Women Who Rape Men," 2014. (Available on Amazon Kindle Books).

until January of 2012.

With the U.S. Department of Justice finally providing a gender neutral definition of rape, we may see accurate statistics, and, accurate analysis of those statistics in the near future.

However, for now, it is clear that the real incidence of rape in the U.S., and globally, is only a small fraction of the rate of rape that is promoted by government offices and the mainstream media.

A CASE STUDY OF MEDIA RAPE HYSTERIA

On May 27, 2014, tragically, two girls about age 14 were found hanging by their necks in a tree in Badaun, India.

Within hours, the international media began a crisis escalation by reporting that the girls had been "gang raped," and, that this was a part of an extensive pattern of sexual violence against women in India, and the rest of the world.

Figure 8 – Falsified photograph, distributed world-wide by mainstream media outlets. The photograph was "photoshopped" by feminist organizations in India and distributed to the global mainstream media to raise hysteria regarding sexual crimes against women in India.

The headlines, accompanied by (falsified photos) declared:

"Teen girls gang-raped and hanged from a tree – police."[39]   (In fact, the police had

---

[39] Bhalla, Nita (29 May 2014). "Teen girls gang-raped and hanged from a tree - police". New Delhi: Reuters. Retrieved

never suspected that the girls had been raped, nor did they ever report to anyone that the girls had been raped).

"Outrage over gang rape, murder of cousins in U.P. village"[40] (In fact, Western news media paid a few hundred people to assemble to make it appear that there was mass concern over the (unfortunate) death of the girls and the purported rape.

"Badaun Gang Rape: Two of the Accused Confess to Crime"[41] (In fact, five men were accused by the parents of the girls of rape, and were jailed, but none of them ever confessed. Eventually, after months of thorough investigations, all charges were dropped against the five men).

On June 2, 2014, the United Nations issued a statement condemning the gang-rape saying: "There should be justice for

---

May 30, 2014.

[40] CK, Chandramohan (30 May 2014). "Outrage over gang rape, murder of cousins in U.P. village". Badaun: The Hindu. Retrieved May 30, 2014

[41] Badaun Gang Rape: Two of the Accused Confess to Crime".Outlook. 1 June 2014. Retrieved 1 June 2014.

families of the two teenage girls ... Violence against women is a human rights issue, not a women's issue. Violence against women is preventable, not inevitable ... The Badaun incident highlights the dangers women in India are exposed to due to lack of toilets." [42] In a statement, Lise Grande, the UN's resident coordinator for India, said, "There should be justice for the families of the two teenage girls and for all the women and girls from lower-caste communities who are targeted and raped in rural India". [43]

On June 4, 2014, Ban Ki moon condemned the rape case and spoke against the violence against women that is spreading across the world. He also condemned the destructive attitude of "boys will be boys". [44]http://en.wikipedia.org/wiki/201

---

[42] Jason Burke, "Indian gang-rape girl's family say they have been threatened with violence," The Guardian, June 3, 2014. http://www.theguardian.com/world/2014/jun/03/india-gang-rape-family-threats

[43] "Indian police use water cannon to end gang-rape protest in Lucknow," The Guardian, June 2, 2014. http://www.theguardian.com/world/2014/jun/02/india-police-gang-rape-protest-lucknow-uttar-pradesh," Times of India, June 4, 2014. http://timesofindia.indiatimes.com/india/UN-chief-Ban-Ki-moon-appalled-by-Badaun-gang-rape-case-demands-action/articleshow/36043470.cms

[44] UN chief Ban Ki-moon appalled by Badaun gang-rape case, demands action, Times of India, June 4, 2014. http://timesofindia.indiatimes.com/india/UN-chief-Ban-Ki-

WHAT REALLY HAPPENED?

What really happened to the two young girls is still not certain. After months of investigations, lie detector tests, forensic studies, multiple autopsies[45] and police investigations by more than three different law enforcement agencies, the only thing that is clear is that the girls died by strangulation but they were never raped or sexually assaulted.[46]

It is possible that the two girls committed suicide.

---

moon-appalled-by-Badaun-gang-rape-case-demands-action/articleshow/36043470.cms

[45] Badaun Case: CBI Exhumes Bodies of Two Girls," New Delhi Television, July 19, 2014;
http://www.ndtv.com/article/india/badaun-case-cbi-exhumes-bodies-of-two-girls-561411

[46] Aditya Kalra, "Forensic Report Complicates India Double Rape Murder Case," Reuters Wire, August 22, 2014 "(Reuters) - Indian federal investigators are analyzing a forensic report that found that two teenage girls, earlier believed to have been raped before they were murdered, were not sexually assaulted."

Because of the hysteria that immediately arose in the international media, five men were arrested and detained for months based on false accusations of the parents. The five men eventually exonerated themselves by all five of them passing lie-detector tests, [47] and, because there was virtually no evidence against them other than accusations by the girls' parents.

In addition, with regard to the accusations of the girls' parents, none of the parents or accusers passed a lie detector test – they all failed. Police suspect the parent accusers, themselves, of having murdered the girls.[48]

What is also clear is that this terrible tragedy had nothing to do with rape, gang-rape, men in general, or any "rape culture" that routinely

---

[47] Sunetra Choudhury, "Badaun Gang-Rape Case: Five Accused Pass Lie Detector Tests, Say Sources" New Delhi Television, August 06, 2014 18:03 IST; http://www.ndtv.com/article/india/badaun-gang-rape-case-five-accused-pass-lie-detector-tests-say-sources-571732

[48] "Main witness in Badaun gang-rape case fails lie-detector test: CBI," Times of India, September 18, 2014. http://timesofindia.indiatimes.com/india/Main-witness-in-Badaun-gang-rape-case-fails-lie-detector-test-CBI/articleshow/42731203.cms

promotes violence against women.

The "gang rape" which received instant world-wide media distribution was nothing more than poor journalism, fraud and hysteria. Most of the fraudulent media stories were disseminated to Western journalists by gynocentric political and media interests who sought to gain political influence, government budget increases and gynosympathy from the falsified rape incident.

India is not a country in which women are at great risk for rape. Nor is it a country in which men are pre-disposed to rape women. Rather, it is a country that exploits rape hysteria to perpetuate a system in which women are privileged, and, in which that privilege accelerates because of the rape hysteria.

Fully, 53% of accusations of rape in India are false, and that figure is conservative based upon estimates from Indian feminist groups.[49] Some

---

[49] "53% rape cases filed between April 2013 and July 2013 false: Delhi Commission of Women." DNA, October 14, 2014; http://www.dnaindia.com/india/report-53-rape-cases-filed-between-april-2013-and-july-2013-false-delhi-commission-of-women-2023334

districts of India have a false rate of rape accusations that exceed 93%.

One of the causes of this rape hysteria, and its vile system of false accusations of rape, lies in the system of Indian government which rewards women for making false accusations of rape. At this time, if any crime occurs whatsoever in which the victim is a woman, it is likely that the woman will accuse someone of rape just so that she can obtain a reward ("victim compensation") from the Indian government of up to $200,000.00.[50] The reward is payable almost immediately upon a woman making an accusation of rape whether the accusation is true or false.

It is likely that this "rape hysteria" is spreading to Western countries. For example, the government paid a woman in California, Wanetta Gibson, for falsely accusing an N.F.L. football player, Brian Banks, of rape. She was eventually caught on video tape confessing that her ac-

---

[50] "Rape Victims in India to Get up to Rs 2 lakh victim compensation," Infochange (Women), http://infochangeindia.org/women/news/rape-victims-in-india-to-get-rs-2-lakh-compensation.html

cusation was false, but, not before Mr. Banks had spent four years in prison for a crime he did not commit.[51]

In conclusion, it is clear, that rape hysteria threatens the integrity of our legal system, and the freedom of individuals to an extent not seen in Western culture from any other form of hysteria in Western history.

Gynocentric interests are intentionally inflaming rape hysteria to empower women, as women of the Ku Klux Klan were empowered during the Jim Crow era, to call for sexual violence against any man simply if a woman chooses to accuse him of rape.

---

[51] "Brian Banks' accuser caught on video confessing that Rape Accusation Was Fake," Huffington Post, June 8, 2012. http://www.huffingtonpost.com/2012/06/08/brian-banks-accuser-caugh_n_1581605.html

CHAPTER 2
Women of the Klan:
Foundations of Modern Feminism

Misandry [hatred of Men and masculinity] is not a new invention in the Story of Humanity. Misandry has been used since ancient times to promote the concept of disposability of men, in the service of women, or in the service of those in power.

This misandry, in the service of gynocentricity, has rarely been more evident than in the Jim Crow era in the U.S. in which women were empowered to dispose of men simply with accusations.

THE INVISIBLE EMPIRE – WOMEN OF THE KLAN

The stereotype of members of the Ku Klux Klan, is of a rural Southern white man who commits random acts of terror and violence against Catholics and African-Americans.

However, almost unknown to the American public, and the world, was a vast organization of Women who subscribed to the values of the Ku Klux Klan, and, who used the sometimes violent arm of the men of the Ku Klux Klan, to promote their agenda for women's suffrage, temperance, and women's supremacy.

These women, numbering in the hundreds of thousands, comprised what was known as "the invisible empire."

Invisible

The Ku Klux Klan is out of politics
henceforth and will carry on work
of an "invisible" nature hereafter,
according to Mrs. Robie Gill Comer,
imperial commander of the women
of the Klan. This picture of her
was taken in Indianapolis, where
25,000 Klanswomen gathered for a
jubilee convention.

The invisible empire, though virtually an almost secret organization, was responsible for
much of the ability of the Ku Klux Klan [KKK], to
infiltrate the legitimate government bodies of
state and federal governments in the U.S. The
agendas of the Women's KKK seemed benign –
they were ostensibly seeking "equality" with men
(in all matters) – the removal of Eurocentric traditions that they believed limited women's roles

in society, and they were seeking values which encouraged a matriarchy to re-build the families that had been ravaged and devastated by war (specifically the Civil War).

CREED OF KLANSWOMEN

WE BELIEVE in the American home as the foundation upon which rests secure the American Republic, the future of its institutions, and the liberties of its citizens.

WE BELIEVE in the mission of emancipated womanhood, freed from the shackles of old-world traditions, and standing unafraid in the full effulgence of equality and enlightenment.

WE BELIEVE in the equality of men and women in political, religious, fraternal, civic and social affairs wherein there should be no distinction of sex.

In fact, the Invisible Empire had the exact same ostensible goals of 19th century feminism – an androgynous "equality" between men and women (in which women were superior and men were disposable).

Unfortunately, however, what the KKK promoted as benign objectives, around lofty and noble images of "equality" was, as modern feminism itself, merely a disguise for gender supremacy.

Figure 9 - The ostensible purposes of the Invisible Empire - women of the Klan - was complete "equality" between men and women, in which women held a sanctimonious role of being superior to men.

In the cold light of history, what emerged from the Women of the Klan, was a pattern of exclusivity and supremacy, especially towards

African-American Men and Catholic Men (specifically Hispanic men). It is a pattern that continues, today, in the realities of modern feminism and its pervasive influence over government, media and social constructs.

In her doctoral thesis, Dr. Sarah Elizabeth Doherty, of Loyola University Chicago, has uncovered the real agenda of Women of the Klan, and their pervasive influence within the Ku Klux Klan itself. In her work: "Aliens Found in Waiting: Women of the Ku Klux Klan in Suburban Chicago, 1870-1930: [Women of the Klan deemed anyone who was not a member of the Klan to be an "*alien*."]

The KKK never resolved gender issues that were complicated by female sympathizers seeking a more active role in Klan activities. Rhetoric of the Reconstruction-era Klan called upon white Protestant men to protect and guard the virtue of white womanhood against the threat of freed slaves and carpetbaggers from the North. The language in 1920s Klan publications, in terms of women, focused on the importance of motherhood and the duty of Protestant women to promote the ideals of American citizenry as interpreted by the Ku Klux Klan. Female supporters of the Klan were active in social movements such as suffrage and temperance and became accustomed to involvement outside the home in clubs and or-

ganizations.12 Though Klan officials wanted to find a place for women within the Invisible Empire, they envisioned women in an auxiliary subordinate role. By the time serious consideration was given to the creation of a women's division of the KKK, many women's organizations with related creeds and agendas to the men's Klan already existed. Similar purposed groups included the Ladies of the Cu Clux Clan, Ladies of the Golden Den, Ladies of the Golden Mask, Queens of the Golden Mask, Ladies of the Invisible Eye, Kamelia, Grand League of Protestant Women, Order of American Women, Dixie Protestant Women's Political League, Hooded Ladies of the Mystic Den, Women's Krudaders, Puritan Daughters of America and Ladies of the Invisible Empire or "Loties."13 Klan leadership favored the creation of a new women's organization to be called the Women of the Ku Klux Klan to cooperate with and complement the mission of the men's order.14[52]

---

[52] Footnotes reproduced here from original thesis: [11] Baker, Gospel According to the Klan, 136-39. [12] See Blee, "Joining the Ladies' Organization" in Women of the Ku Klux Klan, 101-22. [13] Ibid, 25-7. [14] "Report of Women of the Ku Klux Klan" [c. 1924], 110-13, Collections of the Indiana Historical Society.

However, behind the mask of "chivalry" and "equality," in step with the main branches of the Ku Klux Klan, the women of the Invisible Empire sought to use brutality, intimidation, lynchings, cross-burnings, torture and political corruption perpetrated by the Klan's "Ghouls" and "White Knights." The "Ghouls" and "White Knights" of the Klan, much like male feminists today, enabled the Women of the Klan to seek power over men, in society, especially men who were not "White Protestants."

(Among other facets of modern society, we have only to look at the huge numbers of African-American men imprisoned in the United States, today, to understand that the Invisible Empire, over a period of a century and a half, has succeeded, with feminism, in demonizing African-American men, in particular, and men in general).

One learned treatise on Women in the Klan, explains the real purpose behind the "Invisible Empire." In "Women of the Klan: Racism and Gender in the 1920's," noted feminist author Kathleen M. Blee writes:

> *For thousands of native-born white Protestant women . . . , the women's Klan of the 1920s was not only a way to promote racist, intolerant, and xenophobic policies but also a*

social setting in which to enjoy their own racial and religious privileges. These women recall their membership in one of U.S. history's most vicious campaigns of prejudice and hatred primarily as a time of friendship and solidarity among like-minded women. But the Klan's appeal to this Indiana woman was not based purely on racism and nativism.

In an effort to recruit members among women newly enfranchised in the 1920s, the Klan also insisted that it was the best guarantor of white Protestant women's rights. The political efforts of a women's order, the Klan claimed, could safeguard women's suffrage and expand women's other legal rights while working to preserve white Protestant supremacy. [53]

(One has only to look at the well-documented and vitriolic campaign of modern feminism, against Catholicism, and the Catholic Church, and Men's equality organizations, to understand that modern feminism is merely the extension of the "Invisible Empire" into the 21st Century).

---

[53] Kathleen M. Blee, Women of the Klan: Racism and Gender in the 1920s (Kindle Locations 37-39). Kindle Edition.

Figure 10 - Feminists of the group "FEMEN" appear at the Vatican to express their hatred for Catholics and Catholicism. This tactic is similar to the repulsive and ostentatious tactics of the anti-Catholic KKK.

This book explores the parallels between the Invisible Empire and modern feminism, and shows how modern feminism is an extension of the principles of the Ku Klux Klan, its supremacy and exclusivity, and its pattern of using violence against men, disguised as "justice," to invalidate real notions of "equality" between men and women.

EARLY HISTORY OF GYNOCENTRIC[54] CHIVALRY AND THE KLAN

The name "Ku Klux Klan" derives from the Attic Greek concept of κύκλος (pronounced: koó-klos, hence koó-klos clan or KKK). Literally, κύκλος

---

[54] *Gynocentric*, Syllabification: gy·no·cen·tric ADJECTIVE: Centered on or concerned exclusively with women; taking a female (or specifically a feminist) point of view. Oxford English Dictionary (2014).

means "cycle." It refers to the concepts of a cycle of governance that was identified by Plato in "The Republic" in Chapters VIII and IX. In Plato's view, the cycle of governance begins with democracy, and inevitably degenerates into oligarchy, then tyranny.[55]

Immediately after the immense tragedy of the American Civil War, the defeated South viewed the government in Washington, D.C., under President Abraham Lincoln, as a tyranny.

In response to that perceived tyranny,

---

[55] But see, Doherty, Sarah Elizabeth, "Aliens Found in Waiting: Women of the Ku Klux Klan in Suburban Chicago, 1870-1930, doctoral thesis, Loyola University (2012). "The name was derived from the corruption of the Greek word "kukloi" or "kuklos" meaning a band or circle of brotherhood. The Klan portion of the name was added later for effect and spelled with a "k" for uniformity. Another theory for the origins of the name is that it was derived from the name of the Aztec Mexican "god of light" or "Cukulan." 30,000 men from Tennessee volunteered for the Mexican War and were feasibly exposed to ancient Aztec folklore and culture. The "knights" portion of the name was later added to accompany the imagery of crusading knights printed on Klan propaganda pamphlets and tracts."

Southerners, on December 24, 1865, gathered in a law office in Pulaski, Tennessee, to form the KKK.

Figure 11 - The actual building at which the KKK was formed on Christmas Eve, 1865, in Pulaski, Tennessee

An account of the formation of the organization is contained in a very rare manuscript known as "The Authentic History of the Ku Klux Klan" by Susan Lawrence Davis (1924). Ms. Davis recounts the actual formation of the KKK in her semi-autobiographical account. Ms. Davis was an eye-witness to the formation of the Klan.

During the evening the organization was

perfected. Captain John B. Kennedy, on the committee to select a name mentioned one which he had considered, "Kukloi," from the Greek word "Kuklos," meaning a band or circle. James R. Crowe said "Call it Ku Klux," and no one will know what it means. John C. Lester said: "Add Klan as we are all Scotch-Irish descent."

He then repeated the words: "Ku Klux Klan," the first time these words ever fell from human tongue. The weirdness of the alliteration appealed to the mysterious within them; so the name was adopted with a feeling that they had chosen something which would excite the curiosity of their friends and carry out their idea of amusement, which, most unexpectedly to them, proved a boon to Pulaski and the South.

James R. Crowe suggested to make it more mysterious, that a costume be adopted. They then made a raid upon Mrs. Martin's linen closet and robed themselves with boyish glee in her stiff linen sheets and pillow-cases, as masquerading was a popular form of entertainment in those days. Wishing to make an impression they borrowed some horses from a nearby stable and disguised them with sheets.

Figure 12 – From the American film "Birth of a Nation" 1915. The KKK was organized as "an institution of chivalry." Modern feminism is dependent on feudal "chivalry" for its political and societal power.

The precepts of the Ku Klux Klan (KKK) are clear in its originating documents promulgated in 1868. The KKK ". . . is an institution of chivalry . . . . embodying in its genius and its principles all that is chivalric . . . ." [*Id.*]

But what did the founders of the KKK consider to be "chivalry?"

To answer that question, it is necessary to reach into the past about 1,000 years.

Chivalry began roughly around the turn of the first millennium (about 1,000 A.D.). Not coincidentally, this time period saw a large amount of hyper-aggression among European feudal lords, seeking to increase their power, wealth and military influences. These same feudal lords, some pretending to be kings and emperors, sought excuses to enter the crusades for the ostensible purpose of reclaiming the Holy Lands from Islam. In reality, however, their purpose was to increase their ability to plunder neighboring kingdoms, Middle Eastern civilizations, and increase their stores of gold and slaves.

It is during this period of slavery, hyper-aggression, militarism, plunder and incessant feudal conflicts, that the Klan's notions of "chivalry" evolved into what it was at the turn of the 20th Century in the U.S.

Feudal chivalry was marked by one distinguishable characteristic. Men were considered disposable, in combat or otherwise, in the service of women, who were elevated to a special sanctity and protected status. (Not unlike their status under modern feminism).

The turn of the first millennium saw a change in European culture's views of women. With the assistance of the Church, women were elevated to a special status because of their abilities to give birth (to replenish the supply of soldiers (cannon fodder) needed for feudalism), and, as being necessary to provide heirs to thrones and feudal holdings.

Below is a diagram of the process by which women underwent a positive re-evaluation of what Charlemagne's court would term: *La querelle des femmes* ("the question of women" [and their role in society]). Women's roles, as a collective gender, evolved from being mostly slaves (owned, like men, by the state) to a new level of sanctity requiring the solicitous chivalry and gallantry of men for their protection and succor.

Men were relegated to their roles as disposable defenders of the realm, and, the women who ruled over the realm.

Feudalism created a structure of "civilization" in which men were given grandiose titles, and lofty positions of supposed power. This gave the illusion that men were the ones who controlled civilization. The reality of feudalism, however, was that men were pledged from birth to be in service of women; women retained the right to life and to be "defended" at the expense of the lives of men; and women retained more powers over property, civil discourse and sexuality, while they were safe at home than the men being slaughtered on the battlefields.

Figure 13 – (tapestry) Eleanor of Aquitaine as leader of the Second Crusade (in which hundreds of thousands of men died to increase her power and wealth).

This became clear during the reign(s) of Eleanor of Aquitaine.

Eleanor of Aquitaine (1137-1152) was one of the most powerful and influential figures of the Middle Ages. Inheriting a vast estate at the age of 15 made her the most sought-after bride of her generation. She would eventually become the queen of France, the queen of England and lead a crusade to the Holy Land. She is also credited with establishing and preserving many of the courtly rituals of chivalry.[56]

---

[56] http://www.history.com/topics/british-history/eleanor-of-aquitaine

The 12th century intersection of cultural factors that created the gynocentric cultural complex (GCC) and subsequent timeline of events

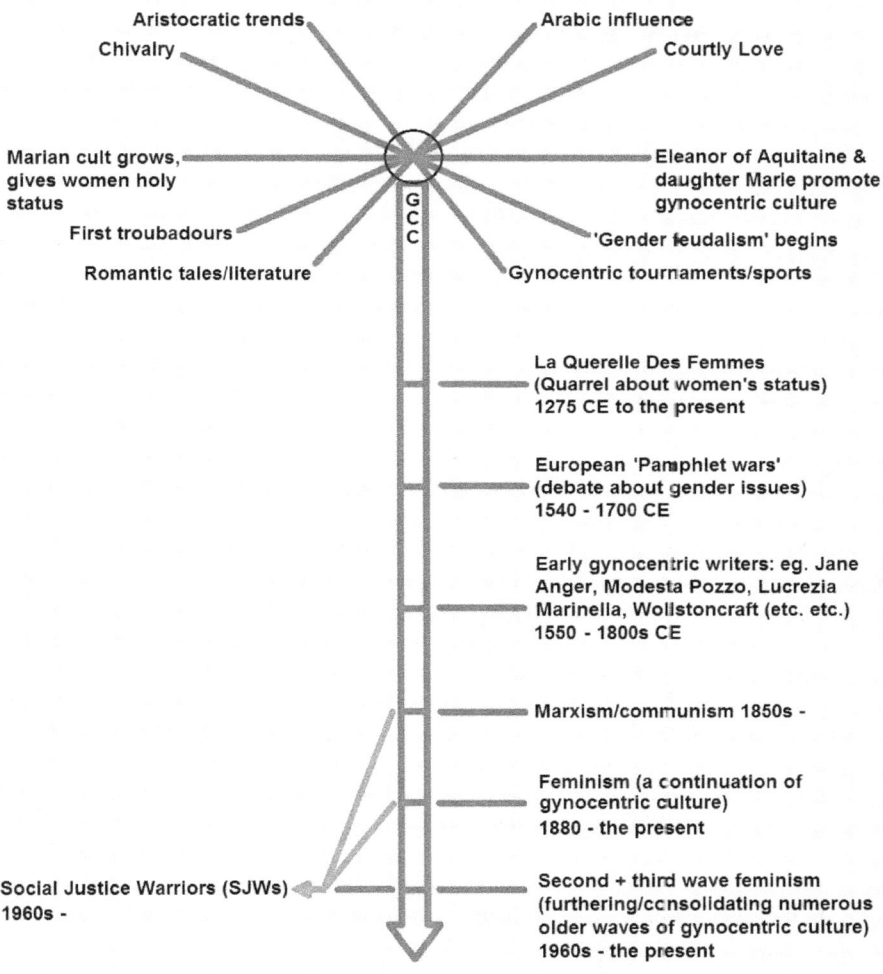

Figure 14 – The creation of the Gynocentric Cultural Complex (GCC). Diagram courtesy of: Peter Wright.

"Courtly rituals of chivalry" refers to an actual court system, presided over by Eleanor of Aquitaine herself, her daughter Marie . . . and sixty other women (but not a single man). They were known as *"les cours d'amour"* - "The Courts of Love."

This amounted to little more than state-sponsored feminism. In this "court" system, Eleanor, a woman, and sixty other women were the sole arbiters of customs between men and women engaged in intimacy.

If a woman felt aggrieved by her lover, she would bring her complaint to the Court and either Eleanor, or Marie, or other high-born women would "resolve" the dispute. The queen's resolutions were enforceable by means of the queen's command over state violence. They were also enforceable through severe social sanctions such as shunning.

In addition, literary poets and troubadours of the time, spread gynocentric viewpoints of the powerful Queen Eleanor all across Europe. The literary poets and troubadours were the "mainstream media" of the time. The gynocentric judgments of *les cours d'amour* (the courts of love), coupled with Eleanor's political power as Queen of both France and England, insured that the gynocentric attitudes of the Poitevin Code [the courts of love were located in Poitiers in the South of France] became the law and the prevailing gender attitudes across most of Europe.

What were the codes of the courts of love? The most accurate statement comes from a scholar writing in 1937 in a well-respected journal article. Writing in Speculum: A Journal of Mediaeval Studies (January, 1937), Amy Kelly writes:

"In the Poitevin code, man is the **property**, the very **thing** of woman. . . ."[57]

Chivalry, therefore, had little or nothing to do with equality between men and women. Chivalry became modern feminism, in which men are merely "disposable property and things," for women who want to "have it all."

This "Court of Love," and the Poitevin code, evolved over the ensuing 800 years into what we

---

[57] Kelly, Amy. "Eleanor of Aquitaine and Her Courts of Love." 12.1 SPECULUM: A JOURNAL OF MEDIEVAL STUDIES 14 (1937).

now know as the "system of family courts." Although there are many male judges presiding over our system of "family courts," those males have been subjected to 800 years of gynocentric conditioning and modern feminism. As a result, current "family courts" isolate most Fathers from their children, strip the Fathers of their assets and income (through alimony, property distributions and child support) and routinely seize children to be placed into the "foster home" or adoption system of the State pending the award of sole custody to the mother.

Nothing could be more pleasing to modern feminism than this wholesale destruction of the nuclear family by the state. To quote one modern feminist, Linda Gordon:

> *"The nuclear family must be destroyed, and people must find better ways of living together.... Whatever its ultimate meaning, the break-up of families now is an objectively revolutionary process....Families will be finally destroyed only when a revolutionary social and economic organization permits people's needs for love and security to be met in ways that do not impose divisions of labor, or any external*

roles, at all."[58]

However noble chivalry may have been considered in medieval times, what is clear is that modern feminism has used the obligations men feel to be "chivalrous" in a way that imposes only burdens and responsibilities on men, and bestows lofty rights and privileges on women. The concept of chivalry has now evolved (or corrupted) to impose unwarranted and unnecessary privileges upon women, solely at the expense of men.

Writing in "The Fraud of Feminism" Ernst Belfort Bax wrote about the feminist view of chivalry:

> *It is plain then that chivalry as understood in the present day really spells sex privilege and sex favouritism pure and simple, and that any attempts to define the term on a larger basis, or to give it a colourable rationality founded on fact, are simply subterfuges, conscious or unconscious, on the part of those who put them*

---

[58] Linda Gordon, "Functions of the Family," Women: A Journal of Liberation (Fall 1969).

forward. [59]

Although Bax wrote that epiphany over 100 years ago, it is still "spot on" today. Feminists refer to it as the "Chivalry Hypothesis." The chivalry hypothesis predicts that women will receive special, privileged treatment in societal constructs, while men will be relegated to positions of disposable convenience for society (some call it: "involuntary servitude."]

For example, men in the U.S. have less rights to vote than women. Under the U.S. Selective Service Act, each man, when he attains eighteen years of age, must register for the compulsory draft in the U.S. for compulsory military service. Women are exempt from this requirement. If men fail to register for compulsory military service, they are denied the right to vote. Outrageously, they are denied the right to apply for student loans, to obtain government financing, to work for the government, and are subjected to a host of other punishments from which their

---

[59] Bax, Ernst Belfort, *The Fraud of Feminism*, Chapter V (The Chivalry Fake), London (1913).

sisters are immune.

In the corrupt judicial system in the United States, there exist numerous sexist laws that deny men rights equal to women. None is more pronounced than the "Violence Against Women Act." This law was originally adopted in Congress (at the fanatical assistance of the now Vice President Joe Biden) to worship the myth that men who beat their wives are so common that a federal law was necessary to address the issue.

The result was atrocious discrimination against men. The Act requires to the police responding to an emergency call involving domestic violence to make an arrest if there is any evidence of violence against a woman. Although the law is conveniently worded so as, *"de jure"* [by law] the police should also arrest the women if there is any evidence of violence against the man, because of the myth of "wife beaters" and rank misandry in U. S. culture, 98% of the time there is mutual domestic violence, only the man is arrested and the woman is immune. This is known as *"de facto"* [in fact] discrimination – although the law, on its face, does not discriminate against men, the way the law is applied, in fact, is perniciously discriminatory against men.

These gynocentric constructs were exactly

what were contemplated by early feminists, by modern feminists, and by the KKK.

By 1925, the KKK had openly adopted a feminist (gynocentric) agenda (stated in the archaic language of the time). For example, the 1925 manual of the KKK called for men who were "White Knights" to follow a code of gynocentric principals. "White Knights" were known as "Ghouls" and were not uncommonly charged by the KKK with lynching, torturing and brutalizing men at the mere accusation of women. In current paradigms, perhaps not coincidentally, men who "chivalrously" impose violence on other men to please women and feminists are known in common language as "White Knights." Not coincidentally, the ghouls of the Ku Klux Klan, who violently enforced the "chivalry" of the Klan upon the rest of the world in order to "defend" "virtuous womanhood."

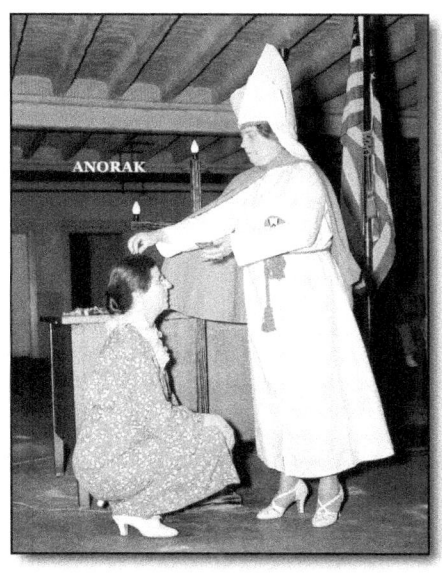

The modern "White Knights" include America's domestic police forces who are some of the most aggressive, militaristic, violent, racist, sexist, and misandrist organizations in the world.

The fierce directives of the Klan, to brutalize other men (especially Catholic men and African-American men) for the sake of "virtuous womanhood" were not unlike the current laws requiring police to make mandatory arrests of men in cases of mere accusations of domestic violence, or the current draconian actions of universities against male students who are merely accused of sexual misconduct, or, the media "lynch mobs" that destroy any man's character who is merely accused of sexual misconduct in our present day culture.

JOIN THE KKK
Loyal White Knights

Call Us Today (336)
WWW   com
Loyal White Knights of the KKK

Figure 15 - "Ghouls" of the KKK who protect "virtuous wom-
ahood" are known as "White Knights" - men who support
feminism are also known as "White Knights." Note the androgynous characteristic of the "White Knight" in the draw-
ing.

The feminist principles the Klan imposed on
its Ghouls included the following:

*"It is the sworn duty of "the Ghouls" to
serve as a chivalrous army for protecting*

'noble womanhood' and that no one could rise above women."

"Womanhood. The Knights of the Ku Klux Klan declares that it is committed to "the sacred duty of protecting womanhood"; and announces that one of its purposes is "to shield . . . the chastity of womanhood."

"The degradation of women is a violation of the sacredness of human personality, a sin against the race, a crime against society, a menace to our country, and a prostitution of all that is best, and noblest, and highest in life. No race, or society, or country, can rise higher than its womanhood..."

Figure 16 – "No race, or society, or country, can rise higher than its womanhood..."

"11. Major Offenses [of Klan doctrines and precepts]

"Major offenses shall consist of...

3. "Disrespect of virtuous womanhood.""

Figure 17 - The Klan ideal of "virtuous womanhood." Note the absence of the Father of the child. It is characteristic of modern feminism to eliminate men from a "family" and alienate the Father from the family.

These exact precepts were, in fact, the same

precepts promulgated by early suffragettes and feminists. They are the tenets of modern feminism in the 21st Century.

False Accusations of Rape:

Modern feminists, in a manner identical to their "sisters" in the 19th and 20th Century Ku Klux Klan, are intensely covetous of womyn's rights to falsely accuse a man . . . any man . . . of rape.

The horrific crime of rape, as feminists remind us, is not just about sex. It is about power.

Similarly, falsely accusing a man of rape is not just about sex . . . it is about power. It is about the power to accuse. It is about the power to raise the hatred and contempt of an entire society against one single man. It is about the power to hold public trials in the world-wide media. It is about the power to ruin a man's life, in the shade of the hanging tree, without due process.

KKK PREPARE TO EXECUTE JOHN CAMPBELL, A REPUBLICAN, AFTER HE WAS RESCUED BY FEDERAL AGENTS. 1871

A woman accusing a man of rape is the closest thing possible to a witch's curse, in which the mere utterance of words can bring complete ruin, torture and death upon any man the accuser wishes to destroy. A woman falsely accusing a man of rape is the feminist equivalent of rape itself.

For this reason, modern feminists closely guard their ability to falsely accuse men of rape. More than half of rape accusations in the United States are false accusations.

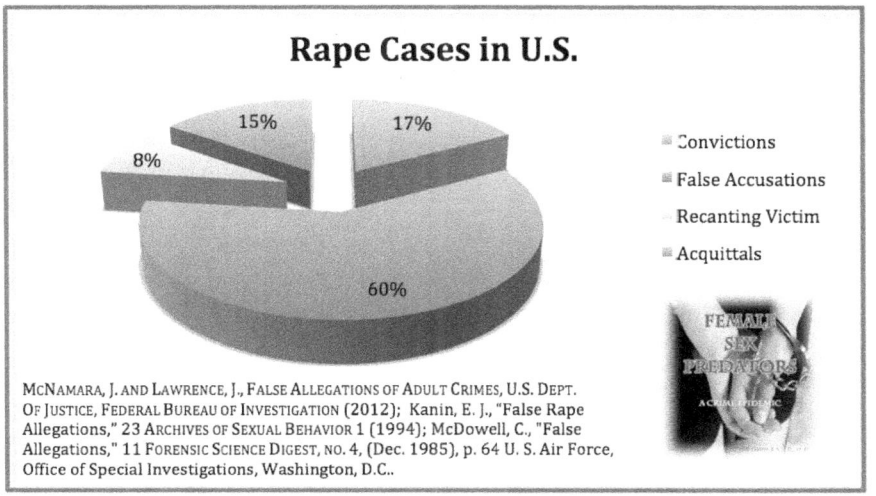

Rape Cases in U.S.

- Convictions
- False Accusations
- Recanting Victim
- Acquittals

17% — 15% — 8% — 60%

McNamara, J. and Lawrence, J., False Allegations of Adult Crimes, U.S. Dept. of Justice, Federal Bureau of Investigation (2012); Kanin, E. J., "False Rape Allegations," 23 Archives of Sexual Behavior 1 (1994); McDowell, C., "False Allegations," 11 Forensic Science Digest, no. 4, (Dec. 1985), p. 64 U. S. Air Force, Office of Special Investigations, Washington, D.C..

Nevertheless, our gynocentric governments, legislators and police forces insist on giving women immunity for making false accusations of rape. The "reasoning" is that if the government punished women who made false accusations, it might deter women who are actually raped from coming forward.

This type of "reasoning" is like saying that we should not punish people who commit murder because it might result in the conviction of people who do not commit murder.

False accusations of rape have, in history, lead to lynchings, torture and tragedy. They continue to result in brutality and false prison sentences for innocent men, while women false accusers are treated with "chivalry" and extended immunity for their crimes.

The crimes of false accusations of rape are a direct result of the corrupt Klan values that are adopted by the legal and judicial system, and the mainstream media, in the U.S.

The Klan's pervasive view of chivalry favoring women, and its corruption of our modern legal system, is no more apparent than it is in the disparity of sentences that men receive in relation to women, for the same crimes.

SENTENCING DISPARITIES BETWEEN MEN AND WOMEN

Michigan State University School of Law, and two independent feminist researchers, recently conducted studies on the sentences women receive in relation to the sentences that men receive.

Professor Sonja Starr of the University of Michigan School of Law, in her recent (2012) paper on gender sentencing disparities, has exposed the blatant racism and misandry in America's judicial system.

In "Estimating Gender Disparities in Federal Criminal Cases," [click on link] Professor Starr noted that in the federal court system, it is common for judges to sentence men prison for three times longer, on the average, than women, for the same crimes.

Figure 18 - Professor Sonja Starr - University of Michigan School of Law – "This paper assesses gender disparities in federal criminal cases. It finds large gender gaps favoring women throughout the sentence length distribution (averaging over 60%), conditional on arrest offense, criminal history, and other pre-charge observables. Female arrestees are also significantly likelier to avoid charges and convictions entirely, and twice as likely to avoid incarceration if convicted."

In a related paper, released just a few days after her paper on gender based sentencing disparities, Professor Starr also noted that African-American men, who comprise over 70% of the

U.S. prison population, receive sentences almost five times greater than white women for the same crimes.[60]

The results of these studies are clear. The U.S. judicial system has adopted, "hook line and sinker" the racist and misandrist views of the Klan into the official policies and procedures of the judiciary in the U.S.

---

[60] Starr, Sonja & Rehavit, Mari, "Racial Disparity in the Criminal Justice Process: Prosecutors, Judges, and the Effects of United States v. Booker," University of Michigan Law School Scholarship Repository, November 1, 2012.

In the area of sex crimes, the same sentencing disparity exists.

In their paper in the journal FEMINIST CRIMINOLOGY, Randa Embry and Phillip Lyons, two feminist researchers, came to the same conclusions as Professor Starr.

Writing in "Sex-Based Sentencing : Sentencing Discrepancies Between Male and Female Sex Offenders," 7 Feminist Criminology 146 (2012), Embry and Lyons again expose the blatant misandry and racism in our judicial system.

In the area of sex crimes, men receive 3 to 4 times longer prison sentences than women, for the same crimes. In addition, women often escape prison sentences for committing sex crimes, whereas prison sentences are almost mandatorily imposed on men, and, always imposed on African-American men.

Not coincidentally, these sentencing disparities favoring women in criminal sentencing is referred to, by feminists, as the "chivalry hypothesis." According to Embry & Lyons' paper:

> *The chivalry thesis, often referred to as paternalism, is similarly situated. This model maps onto the traditional gender roles of men and women asserting that women are weaker and their actions are not seen as completely valid and almost "childlike." Thus, women should not be held to the same standards as men in the criminal justice system as they are not "fully responsible for their actions" (Rodriguez et al., 2006, p. 320).*

These gender based sentencing disparities are the direct result of the judges in the U.S. adopting a century of Klan chivalry towards women, and, the feminist misandry and racism of those feminist leaders of the 19th and 20th centuries.

At least two prominent leaders of the "Women's Movement," after the civil war, were blatantly misandrist, and racist, and subscribed to Klan principles. These women were among influential national leaders who influenced the government of the U.S. to adopt hatred of men, and specifically hatred of black men, as official policy of the U.S. Government and its system of judges.

ELIZABETH CADY STANTON: "WOMEN ARE INFINITELY SUPERIOR TO MEN."

Elizabeth Cady Stanton, and the honored Susan B. Anthony, publicly demeaned prominent African-American men such as Frederick Douglass. Elizabeth Cady Stanton is often quoted by modern feminists as having said:

"Women are infinitely superior to men."

Figure 19 - Stanton disparaged black men and opposed giving African-American men the vote. She was quoted as saying "Women are infinitely superior to men." Much like modern feminism, she was both racist and misandrist.

Stanton and Susan B. Anthony (honored on a U.S. dollar coin) both openly opposed giving African-American men the vote after the civil war. They openly disparaged men and African-Americans, and formed the National Women's Suffrage Association [NWSA] in 1869.

The NWSA was radical and, at times, terroristic in its approach to disparaging men. Though it was not directly related to the Ku

Klux Klan, many of its objectives were identical to the Klan in terms of denying African-American men the right to vote, and, in disparaging men in general.

Relentless in their attacks on men, Anthony and Stanton became known as "The Belligerent Sisterhood."

In addition to being openly racist and misandrist, Stanton was also openly androphobic. "Women, Stanton said, must not put her trust in man."[61]

We must keep in mind that modern feminism considers these women, who were misandrist, androphobic and racist, to be the heroines of feminism, and among its founders. It is not surprising, therefore, to find modern feminism, disguised in politically correct euphemisms, to continue the racist, misandrist and androphobic attitudes and objectives of early suffragettes and the Women of the Ku Klux Klan.

---

[61] Elizabeth Cady Stanton, qtd. In E. Forner at 115.

MARGARET SANGER – FEMINSIM, RACISM & MISANDRY

"We do not want word to go out that we want to exterminate the Negro population, and the minister is the man who can straighten out that idea if it ever occurs to any of their more rebellious members. [Explaining rationale for using prominent black leaders to advocate birth control and abortion]"   - Margaret Sanger - 1923

Margaret Sanger is one of the heroines of feminism. She devoted her entire life to the establishment and perpetuation of planned parenthood, and, was the founder of Planned Parenthood.

Sanger's campaign to provide women "choice" in matters of procreation was a thinly veiled crusade to use modern science to control the race, national cultural characteristics and gender of civilization. Her dream included the specious nobility of providing women "choice," but, at the same time, included the nightmare of excluding men (especially Catholic immigrants (Hispanics and Irish)) from surviving "choice."

Figure 20 - "I accepted an invitation to talk to the women's branch of the Ku Klux Klan...I saw through the door dim figures parading with banners and illuminated crosses...I was escorted to the platform, was introduced, and began to speak...In the end, through simple illustrations I believed I had accomplished my purpose. A dozen invitations to speak to similar groups were proffered." Margaret Sanger – autobiography.

Sanger's view of men was that they had no purpose in a family other than to assume the disposable role of provider. She also advocated that men should have no role in the decision-making process of family planning. Modern feminism holds this same misandry as one of its principal tenets. Like feminism, and the KKK,

Sanger preached exclusivity in which women were elevated to sanctimonious status, while men were relegated to disposable functions in the concept of "family" and in the designs of the State.

Sanger's view of men in the reproductive process was deprecating to say the least. "Woman must have her freedom, the fundamental freedom of choosing whether or not she will be a mother and how many children she will have. Regardless of what man's attitude may be, that problem is hers — and before it can be his, it is hers alone."

Her misandrist and racist views spread quickly across the continent after, World War I, and she often resorted to alliance with the Ku Klux Klan in order to advance her feminist principles.

Modern feminism has adopted the misandry of Sanger and the KKK in grandiose terms:

> *"So, how do we control men's fertility? Mandatory contraception beginning at puberty, with the rule relaxed only for procreation under the right circumstances (he can afford it and has a willing partner) and for the right reasons (determined by a panel of experts, and with the permission of his designated female partner)."*

"...controlling men's fertility would not be a hard restriction to enforce. The fertility authorities could use a combination of punishments for men who failed to get the implants and for doctors who removed them without proper authorization. The men could be required to adopt one orphan per infraction and rear her or him until adulthood. The doctors, could lose their licenses or, in extreme cases, go to prison."

One might be tempted to presume that this quote was of a fanatical fascist, pronouncing 19th century imperial views on social engineering.

This quote is from a 1997 article in Ms. Magazine, and was written by a modern feminist by the name of Margaret Burk.

Sanger's hatred of men, and her pervasive misandry, is no more apparent than in her own writings. In Chapter XVIII of her book: "Woman and the New Race," Sanger writes:

In all of the animal species below the human, motherhood has a clearly discernible superiority over fatherhood. It is the first pulse of organic life. Fatherhood is the fertilizing element. Its development, compared to that of the mother cell, is comparatively new. Likewise, its influence upon the progeny is comparatively small.

Translated into modern terms, Sanger is saying that men have no role in the human race other than to perform perfunctory fertilization. A reading of her book makes it clear that she views this as a valid premise for denying men any meaningful participation in the reproductive process of humans.

Sanger was a key in the early feminist movement to create a society in which men had no rights, and, in which White Women had no responsibilities. It was a vision that Sanger and early Feminism both shared to create a privileged class of White Women that enjoyed all of the benefits of society without having to contribute anything to society.

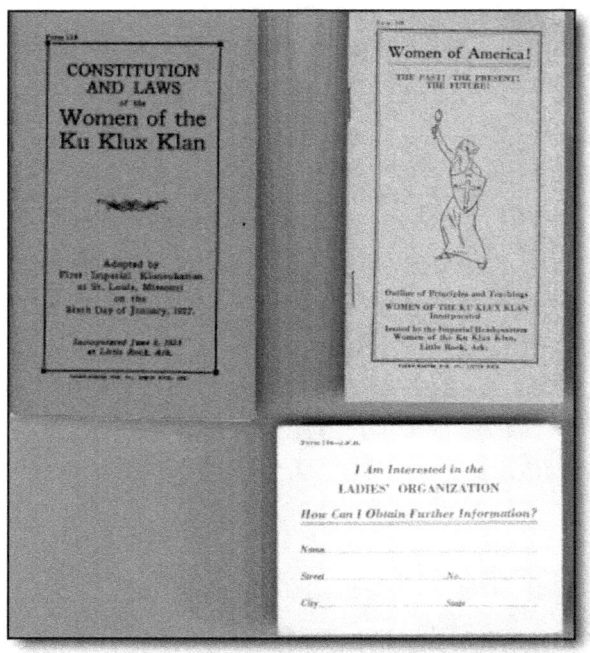

Women were a pervasive influence in the Ku Klux Klan. They molded its policy to conform to 19th century feminist views. By proxy, they used the terror and violence of KKK ghouls as "White Knights" to further their violent agendas against men and African-Americans.

In the 20th century, as the power of the Jim Crow era subsided in the U.S., feminists made it certain that the misandry (man-hating), and racism, of women in the Klan became a pervasive and acceptable official policy of the U.S. Government, its judicial system, and many other governments around the world.

MODERN "JIM CROW:" – THE "IHOLLABACK" INITIATIVE

The term "Jim Crow" refers to a system of enforcing segregation and racism in the U.S. South from the era of the Civil war, to approximately the presidency of John F. Kennedy in the 1960's.

James R. Crow (hence: "Jim Crow") was one of the original founders of the Ku Klux Klan in 1865. Through his influence in the widespread KKK activities of the time, he instituted a set of cultural norms, and corruption of the legal system across the United States, which was intended to keep African-Americans (and other minorities) in a subservient role similar to slavery in the South.

Modern feminism, under the pretense of womyn's "equality," is constantly attempting to institute a new "Jim Crow" system across the United States, and the world. The new feminist "Jim Crow" system would focus on the racism of the Klan, against minority men, but would be used to pass laws structured in such a way that they could entrap any male, and subject those men to arbitrary laws – laws that compel men to be subservient to women.

A classic example is the contemporary feminist drive to make it illegal for men to address a woman, in any manner, while she is in public.

This is known as the "iHollaback" initiative. The iHollaback initiative is a thinly disguised program of apartheid, segregation, racism and misandry.

I DON'T ACCEPT STREET HARASSMENT
I HOLLA BACK

In the autumn of 2014, for the purpose of raising donations, iHollaback created a heavily edited video of a frumpish white woman walking through Harlem in a tight T-shirt, displaying her breasts in a salacious manner. The video was shot only from a front perspective so that viewers could not see the prominent display of her breasts to the minority men in Harlem, or, the tightness of her jeans also displayed to the minority men.

After walking for ten hours, and being filmed, only from the front, the producers claimed that the woman (Shoshana Roberts) had accumulated over 100 incidences of street harassment from men. The remarks included salutations such as: "smile," "have a nice day," how you doing today?," God bless you mami," "you don't wanna talk?," and other common forms of addressing strangers in public.

Figure 21 – Shoshanna Roberts prominently displaying her
breasts in a tight t-shirt, and her hips in tight jeans, soliciting
remarks from minority men in Harlem, in order to "prove"
that men routinely harass women, and, therefore, should be
subjected to criminal sanctions merely for speaking to her.

Many of the remarks that the producers
claimed the men had made sounded as if they
had been edited into the film as opposed to being actual remarks. In some cases, remarks
were edited into the film at points in the film before the men, whom the producers claimed
made remarks, could possibly have seen the
woman in the film.

One woman commentator, Janet Bloomfield, described her manner in the film as "prissy." Prissy (and arrogant) is a fair description of the woman's demeanor in the film. As any resident of Manhattan is aware, such prissy and arrogant behavior, in most public settings, is likely to draw attention and solicit remarks from strangers.

By now, I am sure you have seen this video of a prissy white woman walking the "streets" of New York for 10 hours and being subjected to "harassment". Those words are in quotations because it turns out that the majority of the people saying hello and other inanities took place on one street in Harlem. Princess has rightly been called out for racism and hysteria, forcing iHollaback to issue an apology. "Gee we had no idea targeting men of color would make us look racist". Oh whatever. Nice backpedal there, assholes.

I've written about street harassment before, specifically from the racism angle but today I want to talk about something bigger than just the racial element, although that's still a big part of it. What the iHollaback video, and indeed the entire organization and all that is represents does is contribute to a climate of fear. And not just run of mill, my Spidey senses went on alert fear, but full on hysterical, run away screaming fear.

Fear of what?

Of men. And of black men in particular.[62]

This type of fear is known as "androphobia."

Androphobia is common among feminists and results from cultural conditioning in misandry and racism. It is defined as:

> **androphobia**
> **an-dro-pho-bi-a**: Morbid fear of men, including coming in contact, engaging in activities or becoming intimate with men.[63]

It is iHollaback's intended, and admitted, purpose to instill androphobia in the public in order to raise money, and to provide laws making women a superior class of people to whom men (especially minority men) may not speak. Someone who subscribes to androphobia is

---

[62] http://judgybitch.com/2014/11/10/lets-talk-about-street-harassment/ ["The radical notion that women are adults."]

[63] file://localhost/<a href="http/::medical dictionary.thefreedictionary.com:androphobia">androphobia<:a>

116

known as an androphobe.

an·dro·pho·bic
noun \,an-drə-'fō-bik

Psychiatric Definition
of ANDROPHOBIC

: fear of men : hatred
of the male sex

an·dro·pho·bic *adjective*

Another commentator, writing in U.S. A. Today, recognized how this type of misandrist (man-hating) propaganda is merely the "Jim Crow" South revisited in other areas of the U.S., and applied against all men, instead of just against African-American men.

The commentator, Glenn Reynolds, correctly noted that the video showed only Black men and Hispanic men "harassing" a white woman.

Where were the white guys? The video's producers said they just weren't able to get much good footage of them, for a variety of reasons. Whether, in the 10 hours of filming it took to produce their two-minute video, there just weren't enough white guys saying offensive stuff, or whether the producers just had bad luck or whether they edited out the white guys, the result was that they released a video about "street harassment" that was also, quite plainly, a video of minority men harassing a white woman. And whether or not it deserves the charges of outright racism and classism, or even comparisons to The Birth of a Nation, that it got from some minority critics, that's indisputably what it is.

Mr. Roberts continues in his commentary:

Second, and more troubling, the notion of going after minority males for inappropriate behavior toward white women raises unsettling memories of Jim Crow. Emmett Till, for example, a 14-year-old black youth who visited Mississippi from his home town of Chicago, broke the local behavioral code by flirting with a white cashier while buying some bubble gum. A few days later he was kidnapped, brutally beaten, and fatally shot in the head. An all-white jury, presumably viewing Till's behavior as culpable, refused to convict his killers.

I feel sure, of course, that the makers of today's catcalling video didn't think for a moment about the Emmett Till case, and I am positive that they would not endorse the fatal lynching of the men they pictured. Nonetheless, it's worth noting that the history of controlling minority men's intersexual behavior in this country is closely intertwined with the history of lynching. Those who choose to get involved in this field need to be aware of that history, lest they unintentionally make things worse.[64]

Mr. Reynolds' commentary raises some astute points about modern feminism, and its adoption of Klan principles.

The chivalry of the Klan was to elevate "white women" to semi-divine status. White women (but not minority women) were elevated to a status which conferred on them the right, and unfortunately the ability, to call forth the violence of "white knights," based merely upon their own displeasure and accusations.

Modern feminists seek the same power with government violence. Modern feminists seek to be able to call for police arrests, incarceration,

---

[64] Glenn Harlan Reynolds, " Catcalling a two-way street," USA Today, November 10, 2014.
http://www.usatoday.com/story/opinion/2014/11/03/street-harassment-catcall-video-race-women-gender-equity-column/18373531/

blackballing, censure and ruin of any man they choose to accuse based merely upon their displeasure. Modern feminism has done more to corrupt our current legal system, to erode due process rights of men (especially minority men), than any other corrupting influence in the United States or across the world.

In summary, although comparisons of rituals between the KKK and modern feminism may not be conclusive to establish their similarity, the substantive objectives of both movements are identical – they both seek to create a privileged class of white women, at the expense of oppressing men in general, and minority men in particular.

They are the same union.

Whether we acknowledge the fact, or suppress it, the KKK's influence over the U.S. government, and the modern feminist movement, is undeniable. It continues to this day. It's sole purpose is to create a privileged class of white women who seek unmitigated power to demonize men for their sexuality, and, use that demonization as a pretense for racism, economic advantage for white women, mass incarceration of men, and a fascist legal/judicial system that is devoid of true due process, justice or fairness for common people.

CHAPTER 3
Detecting False Rape Accusations

Science plays a roll in detecting false accusations of rape (as we've seen in Chapter 2).

Unfortunately, proponents of rape hysteria, prefer fear and ignorance to science. It is much easier to misuse the "power to accuse" if science is "shouted down" by angry mobs eager to demonize men for their sexuality. There have been numerous scientific studies on false accusations of rape. Although feminists loudly attack these studies, based upon merely ideological arguments and criticisms, the studies stand as competent scientific bases for addressing false accusations of rape.

One of those studies was conducted in 1985 by Col. Charles P. McDowell, Ph.D. when he was with the U.S. Air Force office of special investigations. Col. McDowell studied 1,218 purported rapes in that were brought to the attention of the U.S. Air Force by female personnel. Col McDowell conducted extensive investigations into each of the claims.

Of the 1,218 claims, his office was able to determine, based upon investigation, that 212 (17%) of the claims were false. In each of the 212 cases in which the accusations were found to be false, the accusing women admitted that the accusations were false.

His investigations then validated about 460 (37%) of the complaints as having some basis in law and fact for a rape complaint.

However, the remaining 546 (44%) complaints were so lacking in evidence as to cast serious doubt on whether they were legitimate accusations of rape.

The Air Force Office of special investigations then proceeded to scrutinize the 546 doubtful cases. Ultimately, in those doubtful cases, 67% of the accusing women admitted that the accusations were false if they were either asked to take a lie-detector test, or, if they had taken a lie-detector test and failed the test.

In response to this scientific study, feminists were successful in passing "rape shield statutes" which prohibited criminal investigators from even requesting that an accuser take a lie-detector test. The sole purpose of these rape shield provisions is to insure that some innocent men will be prosecuted. Because of these rape shield provisions, there is no scientific study to contradict the McDowell study. Consequently, the McDowell study remains one of the two only scientifically based studies on the issue of the frequency of false rape accusations.

Col. McDowell eventually concluded that about 67% of all rape accusations are false, and are not based in fact.

Col. McDowell, being a consummate and qualified scientist, made a thorough study of the cases in which the Air Force, after thorough investigation, was still not able to determine if the case was true or false.

In those shadowy cases, Col. McDowell was able to gather, from the data, various common characteristics among false accusers, and their false accusations of rape.

1. Physical injuries of false accusers usually are limited to superficial cuts, scratches, and abrasions. Scratches often appear in a hatching or crosshatching pattern, due to repeated attempts to make the scratches visible. Scratches that resemble letters or words sometimes are found on false accusers, typically on their abdomens, but are not found on actual victims.

2. False accusers frequently claim that they offered vigorous and continuing physical resistance but suffered no serious reprisals. Most actual rape victims do not offer vigorous resistance, and those who do often suffer extremely brutal reprisals.

3. A false accusation typically solves some perceived problem for the "accuser." It may explain a pregnancy or venereal disease, or it may exact revenge. In contrast, actual rapes seldom appear to solve a problem. They usually create serious problems for the accuser.

4. False accusers usually do not make their allegations initially to authorities. Typically they make them to friends or relatives who in turn inform the authorities.

5. False victims, more often than actual ones, claim to have been raped by strangers.

6. False accusers, much more often that actual ones, claim to have been attacked by multiple assailants who fit an unsavory stereotype (i.e. they claim they were "gang raped.")

7. False accusers typically claim to have been victims of simple penile insertions, or blitz rapes, without collateral sexual activity.

8. False accusers tend to be vague on the details, but when a false victim does provide details she tends to do so with a relish that actual victims seldom have.

9. False accusers, far more frequently than actual victims, cannot say exactly where the rape occurred.

10. In false accusation cases, far more frequently than in actual cases, the purported crime scene and the physical evidence are found to be inconsistent with the allegation.

11. False accusers, more often than actual victims, claim to have received phone calls, or other communications, from their "rapists" before or after the crime.

12. False accusers, more often than actual victims, have personal problems, including difficulty in interpersonal relationships and a history of lying and exaggeration.

It is important to note that the presence, or absence, of any one of these indicators is not, alone, a basis for determining whether a claim of rape is true or false. Taken together, however, as a pattern, the more of the individual items that are present in any given accusation of rape, the more likely the accusation is to be false.

From these studies, Dr. McDowell then compiled an extensive checklist of indices for detecting false rape claims. This checklist provides an excellent basis for quantitatively evaluating, on a numerical basis, the probability that an accusation of rape is false.

Again, it is important to note that no single question or answer in this checklist is determinative of whether a claim of rape is true or false. All of the questions taken together, however, just as if it were a scientific personality inventory, provide an objective index of the probability of the truth of an accusation of rape.

RAPE ALLEGATION CHECKLIST

Created by the US Pentagon and

Charles P. McDowell, Ph.D. USAF, OSI

Initial Complaint Points

1. Was the complaint timely? Y N N=0.5

2. Was the initial complaint made by the victim to a friend? Y N Y=0.5

3. Were law enforcement authorities notified by someone other than the victim? Y N Y=3.0

Nature of the Allegation

4. Does victim report being abducted? Y N Y=0.5

5. Does victim report being intoxicated at the time of the assault? Y N Y=3.0

6. Does victim's recollection of the details of the assault seem overly broad? Y N Y=0.5

7. Does victim report offering vigorous resistance to her assailant? Y N Y=3.0

8. Is victim able to identify or locate the scene of the assault? Y N N=3.0

9. Does victim report passing out or losing consciousness during the assault? Y N Y=0.5

10. Does victim report waking up (or coming to) and finding her assailant engaging in intercourse with her? Y N Y=0.5

11. Does victim have difficulty in describing the sexual details of the assault? Y N Y=0.5

12. Does victim report anal sex (sodomy)? Y N N=1.0

13. Does victim report forced oral sex (fellatio)? Y N N=0.5

14. Does victim's story contain any significant changes in subsequent retelling? Y N Y=2.0

15. Does victim describe the assault in flat, unemotional tones? Y N Y=0.5

16. Does victim describe the assault with a sense of relish or enthusiasm? Y N Y=0.5

17. Does victim report being assaulted at gunpoint? Y N Y=3.0

Suspect Description

18. Does victim report being assaulted by multiple assailants? Y N Y=0.5

19. Does victim report her assailant(s) as being of a different race or ethnic group? Y N Y=0.5

20. Does victim report keeping her eyes closed during the assault (and therefore not able to identify her assailant)? Y N Y=0.5

21. Does victim describe her assailant as having an unsavory appearance? Y N Y=0.5

22. Does victim report her assailant wore a mask? Y N Y=0.5

23. Does victim report her assailant wore gloves? Y N Y=0.5

24. Does victim describe her assailant as a person she knows or who is familiar to her but can't provide a good physical description? Y N Y=3.0

Physical and Medical Evidence

25. Is the crime scene consistent with the story? Y N N=3.0

26. Does victim display any minor sharp weapon injuries (lacerations)? Y N Y=3.0

27. Is the condition of victim's clothing consistent with her story? Y N N=3.0

28. Does victim present bruises from the assault which are inconsistent in color (age) with the time of the assault? Y N Y=0.5

29. Does victim display any cross-hatching scratches to the face? Y N Y=5.0

30. Does victim display shallow scratches to the face, neck, breasts, thighs or stomach? Y N Y=5.0

31. If scratches are present on the face or breasts, do they cross the eyes, lips or nipples? Y N N=3.0

32. Do any lacerations include hesitation wounds? Y N Y=5.0

33. Does victim display any writing on her body allegedly done by the assailant? Y N Y=5.0

Victim's attitude

34. Does victim seem ambivalent toward her injuries? Y N Y=0.5

35. Does victim appear to feign emotions when relating details of the assault? Y N Y=0.5

36. Is victim reluctant to cooperate with law enforcement authorities? Y N Y=0.5

37. When telling about the assault, does victim have difficulty explaining anomalies or inconsistencies? Y N Y=0.5

38. Does victim demand to be treated by a female physician or interviewed by a female police officer? Y N Y=1.0

39. Does victim express a desire to "drop" the whole matter or otherwise indicate she does not want it investigated? Y N Y=1.0

40. Does victim become outraged when asked to corroborate her assault? Y N Y=1.0

41. Does victim try to steer the interview into "safe" topics or those that will engender sympathy? Y N Y=0.5

Assailant's Communications

42. Does victim report receiving obscene phone calls prior to the assault? Y N Y=1.0

43. Does victim report receiving phone calls from the assailant after the assault? Y N Y=1.0

44. Does victim report receiving any kind of written communication from her assailant before, during, or after the assault? Y N Y=1.0

45. If victim has received a written communication, was it a "cut and paste" note? Y N Y=3.0

46. If victim has received written communication, does it contain any kind of rhyming scheme or take the form of poetry? Y N Y=3.0

47. Does victim report being watched (surveilled) by her assailant prior to the assault? Y N Y=0.5

48. Does the victim report being complimented by her assailant during the assault? Y N Y=0.5

Personality and Lifestyle Issues

49. Does victim report engaging in high risk behavior prior to her assault? Y N Y=2.0

50. Does victim have a history of alcohol abuse? Y N Y=3.0

51. Does victim have a history of financial problems? Y N Y=1.0

52. Does victim have a history of mental or emotional problems? Y N Y=3.0

53. Does victim have a significant medical history? Y N Y=2.0

54. Does victim report prior rapes or assaults? Y N Y=2.0

55. Does victim have a history of work-related problems? Y N Y=2.0

56. Does victim have problems in her interpersonal relationships (i.e., with her husband, boyfriend, or others)? Y N Y=3.0

57. Does the allegation solve a problem for the victim? Y N Y=5.0

SCORING SCALE: 0 - 15: EQUIVOCAL
16 - 35: ALLEGATION PROBABLY FALSE
36 - 75: FALSE ALLEGATION
76 + UP: OVERKILL
Interpreting the scaled and weighted responses is not difficult using this system.

The questions are questions that the interviewer or investigator (or prosecutor) should ask regarding the case, based upon all of the available evidence. Depending on whether the answer to the question is a yes, or a no, then the appropriate score is entered for the question.

For example, if an accuser has a history of alcohol or substance abuse (question 50), then the answer to the question is "Yes" and the score for that question is a "3.0." If the answer is "No" then the score for that question is a "0."

Adding up all of the positive number scores yields the score for the entire list. If the score is between 0 and 15, then, the accusation may be true (further investigation may be appropriate). If the score is between 15 and 36, then the accusation is probably false, but, may still be true. If the score is over 36, then, the accusation will be false (absent clear and convincing contravening evidence).

This excellent evaluation technique can assist law enforcement and prosecutors in evaluating cases in which they are doubtful as to the veracity of the accusation.

This evaluation technique can be helpful to prosecutors and law enforcement officers in evaluating whether a dubious case does, or does not, have sufficient indices of reliability to support an agency finding of probable cause to make an arrest.

The National Center for Women & Policing has compiled a twenty-nine step index of attributes of false rape accusations. Although this office is an advocacy group, it is one of the few advocacy groups that will even admit that false accusations of rape are a significant factor in the challenges that law enforcement faces.

These 29 indices are similar to the indices presented by Dr. McDowell through the Air Force Office of Special Investigations.

TWENTY NINE INDICATORS OF FALSE ACCUSATIONS

1. The falsely accused will often be "a stranger, a "slight acquaintance," [or] a "friend of a friend."

2. The false accuser will often claim "to have fought with all their ability. They typically report punching, kicking, and scratching their assailants until they are themselves finally overpowered."

3. The false accuser will likely "bolster an inability to resist by claiming they were attacked and raped by more than one person."

4. The "pseudo-victim claims the assailant was exceptionally large or powerful and able to overcome her resistance with relative ease."

5. A false accusation will "include the face-saving element of either having resisted or having

been confronted with a situation that made resistance impossible."

6. "The report of rape is not seen by false claimants as requiring collateral reports of oral or anal sex, unless such acts are included in the person's sexual repertoire."

7. "Under-describing of the attack may be another manifestation of the false claimant's naiveté as to what actually occurs in these crimes."

8. "Women who make false allegations seem to more frequently report that they had their eyes closed at the time, that they "passed out" and do not recall the penetration, or that they cannot recall the specifics of the actual sex act itself."

9. "The accuser "may also provide an emotionless, but exquisitely detailed, description of the event. She must either "invent" the acts she alleges, or she must convert a consensual sexual experience into a "rape." Unable to recount objectively something that was done to her, she tends either to become vague and evasive or to cross the cultural barrier and become overly descriptive."

10. "False complainants do not usually present serious physical injuries."

11. "However, as one moves along the continuum of personal pathology, the extent of self-inflicted harm can increase."

12. "False victims who have injured themselves tend to exhibit an unusually wide array of wounds. In spite of this, extremely sensitive organs or tissues such as the eyes, nipples, lips, or genitalia are almost never injured."

13. "Characteristic of pseudo-victims who injure themselves is their tendency to be strangely indifferent to their wounds. They appear to accept their injuries with a degree of nonchalance not found in people who sustain similar injuries at the hands of others."

14. "The consistency or inconsistency of the evidence may suggest that a rape complaint has been exaggerated or is completely false. An absence of the kinds of evidence usually associated with rapes can sometimes be as revealing in identifying false allegations as its presence is in establishing that a rape has actually taken place."

15. "Complainant cannot recall where the crime took place even though she does not report being blindfolded, under influence of drugs or alcohol, or moved from location to location."

16. "Crime scene does not support story."

17. "Damage to her clothing is inconsistent with any injuries she reports (i.e., cuts or scratches inconsistent with tears or cuts in clothing)."

18. "Complainant presents cut-and-paste letters allegedly from the rapist in which death or rape threats are made."

19. "Note or letter is identifiable with pseudo-victim (via handwriting analysis, indented writing, typewriter comparison, paper stock, or fingerprint comparison)."

20. "Confirming laboratory findings are absent."

21. "In false rape allegations, extensive and important information on the complainant is often available. In general, this information suggests that the pseudo-victim has experienced numerous personal problems and that her ability to cope is seriously impaired."

22. "In temporal sequence, the "rape" follows one or more escalating incidents revealing difficulties in her personal relationships."

23."Complainant has history of mental or emotional problems."

24. "Complainant has previous record of having been assaulted or raped under similar circumstances."

25. "Allegation was made after a similar crime received publicity (suggesting modeling or "copy-cat" motive in which the similarity to the publicized crime offers credibility)."

26. "Complainant has extensive record of medical care for dramatic illnesses or injuries."

27. Friends or associates report that the complainant's post-assaultive behavior and activities were inconsistent with her allegation.

28. Complainant becomes outraged when asked to corroborate her victimization.

29. Complainant tries to steer the interview into "safe" topics or those that tend to engender sympathy.[65]

Most feminist critics of these useful inventories pervert the content and application of them to real life situations involving suspected false rape accusers.

Gynocentric propaganda seeks to discredit

---

[65] National Center for Women & Policing, 29 Indicators of False Accusations,
http://www.womenandpolicing.org/aboutus.asp

these inventories (precisely because they are so effective in exposing false accusations of rape) by misstating their content and purposes. These propaganda sources will focus on one of the questions, distort what the question asks, then try to make the entire survey seem ridiculous by claiming that only one of the questions serves as a basis for exposing false accusations.

This survey, like the McDowell survey, requires that a substantial number of the indices be present before one can become confident that an accusation of rape is false. One question, out of the 29 indices, does not, in and of itself, represent a valid detection of a false accusation of rape. However, the more of the indices that are applicable to a particular accusation of rape that appear in a case, the higher the probability that the accusation is a false accusation of rape.

One of the advantages of the National Center for Women & Policing criteria is that it is possible to apply them without direct access to the victim for questioning.

Media rape hoaxes are common means of raising Rape Hysteria in the public. Many of the criteria for false accusations of rape, detailed by the National Center for Women & Policing, are helpful in distinguishing rape hoaxes in the media.

For example, the world was recently ignited into rape hysteria by means of an article in Rolling Stone Magazine about a "gang rape" that purportedly occurred on the University of Virginia campus involving a fraternity.

For weeks, mass media used the story, and the resulting rape hysteria, to call for a lynch mob mentality in the U.S. regarding men who were accused of rape. Calls went out to "believe the victim (accuser)" and to end the "rape culture" that pervades U.S. college campuses.

In the middle of this rape hysteria, some ethical and competent journalists began to question the credibility of the sensational gang rape story in Rolling Stone. The result was the exposure of a shameful disgrace that typified the epitome of rape hysteria, and lynch mob mentality, that is so prevalent in the U.S. and around the world.[66]

---

[66] Glenn Harlan Reynolds, "*The great campus rape hoax: Column,*" USA Today, December 15, 2014. http://www.usatoday.com/story/opinion/2014/12/14/campus-rape-uva-crisis-rolling-stone-politics-column/20397277/

Journalists noted, in their discussion of the hoax article, that many of the "victim" (accuser's) narrative aspects fit the profile of a false accuser as set forth in the National Center for Women & Policing criteria for detecting false accusations of rape.

Had journalists applied these criteria, before publishing the hoax rape story in Rolling Stone, they might have been able to avoid the rape hysteria that resulted. This rape hysteria, resulting from the Rolling Stone article, is the precise same mechanism which motivates lynch mobs to murder, mutilate, torture and demonize men without due process of law.

This rape hysteria is one of the most critical factors in protecting men accused of rape and sexual assault by extending anonymity to them at very early stages of a rape investigation.

Stop the Hate

" Men who are unjustly accused of rape can sometimes gain from the experience." – Catherine Comins (Chair of Feminist Studies)

THAT IS LIKE SAYING THAT WOMEN WHO ARE RAPED CAN SOMETIMES GAIN FROM THE EXPERIENCE, CATHERINE

No one wins when women lie about rape.

CHAPTER 4
A Call for Anonymity

All lynch mobs, especially those sanctioned by governments, have one thing in common. All of them rely upon the knowledge of the identity of the accused to commit violence on the accused (whether that violence is in the form of a physical arrest, or in the form of a lynch mob).

It is for this reason that we should have strict laws (with felony consequences) prohibiting anyone from identifying an accused as a rapist, or child molester, or perpetrator of sexual assault, unless and until that person is convicted by due process in a competent court of law.

In addition to laws that impose criminal sanctions on people for identifying any accused man as a rapist, child molester or sexual assaulter, there should be practical restraints on the criminal justice system, and on journalists, from allowing the identity of the accused to become known outside of law enforcement circles.

These practical steps should include requiring law enforcement agencies (or administrative agencies such as colleges) to seal any and all accusations or complaints of sexual misconduct. If a college undertakes to adjudicate a claim of rape or sexual assault, it should be precluded, by law, from disclosing the identify of the accused. Colleges do not have the ability (outside of a system of kangaroo courts driven by funding pressures) to make reasonable determinations of complaints of rape or sexual assault. Their determinations should not be made public, and, no person participating in those proceedings should be permitted to make any information public.

Law Enforcement agencies should be prohibited, by law, with criminal sanctions, from disclosing any identity of an accused until he has had the benefit of due process of law, in a court of law. This would eliminate the shameful practice of law enforcement agencies "perp walking" an innocent man in front of the mass media, exposing him to ridicule, calumny or danger from physical violence.

Another limitation that should be placed on any accuser is to require a preliminary hearing for any accusation of rape or sexual assault.

A preliminary hearing is a due process device which is designed to weed out unfounded or false accusations. It is used widely in many jurisdictions. However, it has also been almost eliminated in other fascist jurisdictions such as Colorado.

At a preliminary hearing, the accused is given the opportunity to cross-examine the accuser at an early stage. The state is also required to present a minimum amount of evidence to support the accuser's accusation. At this stage, the prosecution would be required to present any and all evidence it has supporting the accusation. That evidence would have to include any DNA identifying evidence that showed the accused could even be properly named as a defendant. (Women routinely accuse men of raping them, but, DNA evidence obtained from testing prior to an arrest or trial absolves fully 25% of men who are accused of rape. This underscores the pernicious and widespread epidemic of false rape accusations in the U.S.).

This preliminary hearing should also be tied to a bond hearing for the defendant so that any bond, or bail, set on the defendant can be weighted on a scale commensurate with the strength or lack of evidence of the accuser/prosecution.

Such procedural and substantive due process safeguards would likely protect the system, and individual innocent defendants, from many of the repercussions of false accusations that are rampant in the system.

Requiring a preliminary hearing early in a case would also provide the accuser with an opportunity to recant her accusation at an early stage and avoid a lengthy prison sentence for having made a false accusation of rape or sexual assault.

At the preliminary hearing stage, there should also be a statute permitting the defense to move for the accuser to post a bond for any damages in the event the accusations are determined to be false or unsubstantiated. This bond requirement, on the accuser, would be most important in cases in which the accuser's accusation, alone, is presented as the evidence of the accused.

In the vast majority of false accusations of rape, there is no corroborating evidence other than the testimony of the accuser. It would be appropriate to require an accuser, who has no corroborating evidence, to post a bond for damages. The reason it would be appropriate is that legitimate accusations of rape usually have physical evidence on the issue of consent. When a woman does not consent, there are numerous clues, in the form of physical evidence in most cases. If she was restrained, for instance, there is almost always bruising on her wrists or the other limbs that were restrained. If she was threatened with a weapon, there is usually forensic evidence of the presence of a weapon. The absence of evidence on these elements of a sex charge should be a basis for requiring an accuser to post a bond that will reimburse the accused for damages in the event the Court ultimately acquits the man.

What kind of damages can be expected when a woman lies about rape, and, a man is falsely accused? A prominent defense counsel explains:

We are relentless at public shaming and humiliation.

This type of abuse is routinely suffered by lesser-known rape defendants. They are terrorized by the media circus, and turned into carnival freaks. Unruly crowds rally in front of their home. They are followed, spat on, chased through the streets, forced to move, lose their sanity and some even commit suicide to end the abuse. They are the new victims of modern technology: Google, Twitter, Facebook and cable news. The accusation is forever imprinted in cyberspace, only a keystroke away. Reputations are smeared, finances eviscerated, careers destroyed; jobs, businesses, friends, wives and children lost forever. All of this regardless of the verdict.

Does this have to happen? Newsrooms self-regulate to cloak the identity of a rape accuser. Editors understand that the potential harm of naming putative victims outweighs any journalistic reason to publish. But apparently journalist ethics don't extend to the presumptively innocent. We grant the ac-

cuser name suppression due to the stigma attached to rape but, after a gradual, and justifiable shift in our collective consciousness, there now is a far greater stigma for men accused of rape. The Supreme Court called rape "highly reprehensible, both in a moral sense and in its almost total contempt for the personal integrity and autonomy of the female victim." It is a powerful and repulsive charge, and the accused should have their identities protected by law.[67]

The accused's identity should be protected all the way through the trial and appeal phase (if the accused appeals an adverse verdict). This would insure that the identity of the accused would not be available for lynch mobs until such time as the accused was taken into custody, and provided with adequate security, to protect his life from lynch mobs within and without the prison system.

---

[67] Black, Roy, "Why we should protect those accused of rape," Salon, (July 27, 2011); http://www.salon.com/2011/07/27/dsk_kobe_assange_flatley/

CHAPTER 5
Government Sponsored
False Accusations

Another influence on the rapidly expanding epidemic of false rape accusations, is the government policy of paying money to women to make false accusations of rape.

It may be difficult for most Americans (or citizens of other countries around the world) to believe that governments actually pay women to make false accusations, however, the evidence is not disputable.

In first encountering this assertion, most

people reading it will respond with disbelief and fierce denial. The concept itself so contradicts the notions of justice that the average person recoils at the thought that their worshipped government would, or could, be so malignant as to advance false accusations of rape with money taken from taxpayers.

One case study of the government using public money, to encourage false rape accusations, lies in the story of professional football player, Brian Banks.

Mr. Banks, in high school, was a top college football prospect. He played as a middle linebacker at Long Beach Poly High School in Los Angeles. During summer school, he got up from class to make a phone call. While in the hallway, Mr. Banks ran into a high school sophomore by the name of Wanetta Gibson. Gibson flirted with Mr. Banks and the two went to an excluded spot where they engaged in consensual sex. This was in February of 2002.

Shortly after Mr. Banks graduated from high school, Gibson accused him of rape. The California "Innocence Project" describes what happened to Mr. Banks' dreams of being a professional football player.

A high-school acquaintance – Wanetta Gibson – shattered that dream one fateful day after she accused Banks of rape and kidnapping following a consensual sexual encounter on the school campus. It was Banks' word against hers and she was not likely to change her story. After all, Gibson sued the Long Beach Unified School District claiming the school's lax security provided an unsafe environment that led to the fraudulent rape. She would eventually receive a settlement of 1.5 million dollars.

Banks was faced with an impossible decision at the time – either fight the charges and risk spending 41 years-to-life in prison, or take a plea deal and spend a little over 5 years of actual prison confinement. Although it would mean destroying his chance to go to college and play football, a lengthy probationary period, and a lifetime of registration as a sex offender, Banks chose the lesser of two evils when he pleaded no contest to the charges.

Nearly a decade after his conviction, Gibson recanted her statements and has acknowledged she fabricated the whole story. The California Innocence Project pre-

sented this evidence of Banks' inno-
cence to the Los Angeles District At-
torney's Office who launched an in-
vestigation into the case. After a
thorough review of the evidence,
the District Attorney's Office con-
ceded that Banks was wrongfully
convicted.

On Thursday, May 24, 2012,
Judge Mark C. Kim of the Los An-
geles Superior Court reversed
Banks' conviction and ended his
nightmare of wrongful convic-
tion.[68]

Wanetta Gibson was, literally, paid $1.5 Million dollars, by a government entity, to falsely accuse Mr. Banks of rape.

As part of the denial process, many readers will be tempted to declare that the government did not "intend" to pay her to make a false accusation of rape. False rape apologists will "explain" that the government's intent in making

---

[68] http://californiainnocenceproject.org/read-their-stories/brian-banks/?gclid=Cj0KEQiA6ounBRCq0LKBjKGgysEBEiQAZmpv A20gfuOnQaHMpQTdMV11YMCY7is4lYNBotB2ftH4NE0aAuf q8P8HAQ

such payments is to "compensate" a victim for injuries sustained as a victim of crime. This argument, however, is merely pedantic and semantic. However one labels a payment to a false accuser, whether it is "victim compensation," or a "bounty" for making false accusations, the result is the same – Gibson was handsomely rewarded, by government entities (through the government entity of a court system) for falsely accusing an innocent young athlete of rape. That the government was reckless in its funding of the false rape accusations is little different than if it had intended the result of paying Gibson $1.5 M to make a false accusation of rape.

Gibson finally confessed to Mr. Banks, and his private investigator, while being secretly taped, that there had been no rape and that the intercourse between them on that fateful day had been fully consensual. She stated, however, that she was not willing to exonerate Mr. Banks because if she was truthful with the authorities, she may have to give back the $1.5 million dollars the government had provided to her for her false accusation of rape.

Heavy government funding for women to make false accusations of rape is not limited to the U.S. Government. The country of India, for example, is required to pay false rape accusers the moment they make a false accusation of rape. The amount of the payment is up to the equivalent of approximately $212,685.00.[69]

The moment an accuser files a claim for compensation as a "rape victim," whether there is any proof of rape or not, the victim is entitled to receive 20,000 rupees from the Indian government, payable within two weeks of the false accusation of rape being made. More money is paid to the accuser (whether the accusation is true or false) as the case progresses. The accuser is literally paid to testify against the man she has accused, and, receives even more money if the man falsely accused is convicted on the basis of her false testimony.[70]

The result of this government sponsorship, of

---

[69] In terms of real exchange rates, the actual upper limit a rape accuser may receive for making a false rape claim is about $112.685.22 USD. Although a modest sum in the U.S., it is a royal fortune for anyone residing in India. It is at least comparable to the 1.5 Million USD payment that Wanetta Gibson received for her false accusations against Mr. Banks.

[70] Editorial, "*Rising Menace of False Rape Cases in India Problems and Solutions*," 35 J. INDIAN ACAD. FORENSIC MED. 3, Juu-September 2013.

false rape accusations, is that the rate of false rape accusations in India have climbed to as much as 93% in some districts. In addition, the acquittal rate in cases that eventually go to trial (while the falsely accused are in prison) have reached as high as 73% in major metropolitan districts such as New Delhi.[71] Of the remaining 47% of cases which proceeded to trial, 78% of those cases turned out to be false cases as well, resulting in acquittals.[72]

As a result of the government funding of false accusations of rape, rape hysteria has taken hold in India, as it has on college campuses in the U.S., and in the worldwide mainstream media.

---

[71] *Id.* Even the Delhi Commission for Women (DCW), an anti-male feminist group in India, admits that 53% of cases filed in New Delhi were false cases. http://www.dnaindia.com/india/report-53-rape-cases-filed-between-april-2013-and-july-2013-false-delhi-commission-of-women-2023334

[72] MAHENDER SINGH MANRAL, "False rape' cases soar in Delhi as number of acquittals hits 78 per cent," Daily Mail India, June 12, 2014. http://www.dailymail.co.uk/indiahome/indianews/article-2656609/False-rape-cases-soar-Capital-number-acquittals-hits-78-cent.html

The argument of false rape apologists is that the government's intent, in providing victim compensation, is not to foster false accusations of rape, but, to compensate victims for harm. This argument is specious (*i.e.* it sounds good but it falls apart under examination). When any person or entity proceeds with reckless[73] disregard for the truth, or, the consequences of their actions, then, they are presumed to be acting with intent to cause the consequences that result. We can infer, especially from the high rates of false accusations of rape, that governments intend to support and cause increases in false accusations of rape, by continuously paying women to falsely accuse men.

It is vital to the interests of justice that governments and institutions begin discouraging incentives to women to falsely accuse men of rape.

---

[73] Reckless means: "Conduct whereby the actor does not desire harmful consequence but...foresees the possibility and consciously takes the risk," or alternatively as "a state of mind in which a person does not care about the consequences of his or her actions." Black's Law dictionary 1053 (Bryan A. Garner ed., 8th ed. abr. 2005).

CHAPTER 6
Conclusions & Recommendations

All of our hope of preserving the ideals of humanity lies in taking actions to discourage lynch mob mentalities. In the area of human sexuality, and especially in the area of men's sexuality, it is critical that we cast off the time-honored superstitions and myths regarding men. It is also time that we cast off the abhorrent propensity of mass media, and collective interests, to promote misandry and the demonization of men and their sexuality.

THERE MUST BE EFFECTIVE LAWS AGAINST WOMEN WHO MAKE FALSE ACCUSATIONS OF RAPE.

Current laws do not effectively address the epidemic of women making false claims of rape against men.

The problem of false accusations, and lynch mob mentality, has been with us for centuries. It needs to stop.

There needs to be criminal statutes that impose real and certain penalties on women for making false accusations of rape, and, which provide society with notice of a woman's propensity for making false accusations. (Many women who false accuse are serial false accusers).

An ideal statute would include a minimum penalty for a false accuser. The statute would encourage a false accuser to recant her false accusation sooner rather than later. The statute would provide for mandatory restitution orders in favor of the victim of the false accusation of rape. Finally, such a statute would ideally require the false accuser to register as a sex offender in local and national databases of sex offenders.

Such a statute might look like this:

18 Stat. § 101: *False Accusations of sexual misconduct.*

(a)   Any person who makes any utterance, publication or statement that states or implies that another person is guilty of rape or sexual assault, knowing that the utterance, publication or statement is false, or, having reason to know that the utterance, publication or statement is false, shall be guilty of a Felony.

(b)   No person (including any government personnel or any other person including judicial persons) shall reveal the identity of any person accused of rape or sexual assault until such time as a court of competent jurisdiction has entered a final judgment, with all appeal rights exhausted, declaring the person to be guilty of rape or sexual assault; any person who violates this section shall be guilty of a Felony.

(c)   There shall be no immunity privileges asserted in response to a charge under subsection (b).

(d)   Any person who violates the provisions of subsection (a) shall serve a term in the state prison not less than any amount of time, including pre-trial confinement, that any falsely accused served as a result of the false accusation.

(e) Any person who violates the provisions of subsections (a) or (b) shall be strictly liable for any damages the falsely accused victim incurs as a result of the false utterance, publication or statement.

(f) Any court entering judgment against a false accuser under this provisions shall award full restitution to any falsely accused, including restitution or damages that arise or become known after any hearing on restitution. A victim of a false accusation of rape or sexual assault may re-open the issue of restitution in any criminal proceeding under this provision, at any time, to seek additional compensation for restitution of damages or injuries.

(g) There shall be no statute of limitations for any charge brought under this provision.

(h) Any person who violates the provisions of subsection (a) or (b) of this provision shall be required to register as a sex offender under any applicable state or federal laws.

(i) Punishment under this provision shall be the minimum prison sentence as specified in subsection (d) up to an including twenty-five years in prison, plus a fine of up to $500,000 or both.

FUNDING FOR LAW ENFORCEMENT & TRAINING:

There should be increased funding for training of law enforcement officers and institutions to provide adequate security for any man accused of rape or sexual assault.

- o Sensitivity to male victims of false accusations;

- o Recognition of female sex predators who have made false accusations;

- o Collection and disclosure of evidence in cases of victims of false accusations of rape if the evidence tends to show, in any way, that the accused is innocent;

- o Training for Law Enforcement Officers and institutions to recognize and disregard advocates and false rape apologists who pressure unfair and untruthful investigations and false rape accusations.

Mr. Black, has also commented on the need for recognizing the pressures driving false accusations:

> *For decades, there has been a unique, growing disparity between the way we treat accused rapists and their accusers. It's grown because of a relentless pressure to manipulate the rules to increase arrests and convictions in rape cases. The protections against false accusations have been whittled away one by one to make it easier to charge and easier to convict, with the unintended consequence of making it easier to make a false accusation.*
>
> *In order to more easily file criminal charges, these basic protections have been eliminated:*
>
> *•A required corroboration of a rape taking place; now, the accusation alone is sufficient*

•Evidence of a clear element of force or the threat of force

•The classic element of mens rea (guilty mind)

And in pursuit of convictions, rolled back protections have included:

•The ability to cross-examine accusers about past conduct. Rape shield laws insulate an accuser's past while creating rules to greatly broaden evidence of the accused's past conduct. (see Fed. Rule Evid. 413 for the most outrageous example.) Even evidence of the accuser's prior false allegations of rape is inadmissible because it is considered sexual conduct within the meaning of the shield statute.

•Intoxication as a defense -- while consent by an allegedly intoxicated victim doesn't matter.

•The cautionary jury instruction that rape is a charge easily made but not easily defended.

We need a modest reform to mitigate these changes. This is not a zero-sum game where a benefit to the accused is detrimental to the accuser. There is an obvious benefit to discouraging false charges and denying the ability to use them as blackmail or as a weapon in domestic disputes.

MINIMUM PRISON SENTENCES IN CASES OF RAPE HOAXES PERPETRATED BY THE MEDIA AND BY JOURNALISTS.

Justice Oliver Wendell Holmes once wrote, in *Schenck v. United States*,[74] that the First Amendment of the United States Constitution does not protect all speech. It does not, for instance, "protect a man falsely shouting fire in a theater and causing panic."

The same ruling should apply to journalists, news media outlets, and individuals who unnecessarily spread the panic that results in lynch mobs.

---

[74] 249 U.S. 47 (1919). Opinion construing portions of the Espionage Act of 1917.

There should be special felony statutes to address the multiple rape hoaxes, for instance, that the mainstream international media has perpetrated regarding India. This should include so called "documentaries" which have the sole purpose of engendering panic and instilling hatred of men and their sexuality in the populace by means of mass media propaganda.

Such propaganda clearly stirs up nothing but mob violence against men in general, and, specific men (many of whom are falsely accused). Such mob violence is conduct that is lower than that of animals and belongs in the category of human conduct that is too vile to describe with words.

There is no question that mass media has the ability to generate lynch mobs, and, worse, to generate serial lynchings.

Rape is a serious crime. Rape, however, does not justify murder, or the death of a man, especially innocent men.

It is time to start imposing criminal liability on journalists and media companies, including prison sentences for media executives, who disseminate hateful media content against men, and their sexuality.

These are the minimum steps we need to take as a civilization to diminish the lynch mobs, in the Twenty First Century, which reduce our humanity, to inhumanity, and which represent the devolution of mankind.

Glossary of Special Terms

Androphobia, Syllabification: an-dro-pho-bi-a (psychiatric) NOUN: A Morbid fear of men, including coming in contact, engaging in activities or becoming intimate with men.[75]

Gynocentric, Syllabification: gy·no·cen·tric ADJECTIVE: Centered on or concerned exclusively with women; taking a female (or specifically a feminist) point of view. Oxford English Dictionary (2014).

––––––––––––––––––––

[75] file://localhost/<a href="http/::medical dictionary.thefreedictionary.com:androphobia">androphobia<:a>

Hypoagency, Pronunciation: /ˈhaɪpəʊ//ˈeɪdʒənsi/
NOUN: Less than appropriate accountability.

Misandrist, Pronunciation: miˈsandrist NOUN: A person who dislikes, despises, or is strongly prejudiced against men: the counterpart to a misogynist is a misandrist. Oxford English Dictionary (2014).

Misandrist, Pronunciation: miˈsandrist ADJECTIVE: Relating to or characteristic of a misandrist: 'the university is teaching misandrist lies' Oxford English Dictionary (2014).

ABOUT THE AUTHOR

John Davis (1953 -) was born in Cleveland, Ohio. He was educated at Case Western Reserve University (BA) (one of the top ten universities in the United States), Seattle University School of Law (JD), and, New York University School of Law (LL.M post-doctoral) (one of the top ten law schools in the United States). John is fluent in seven languages (including ancient Latin and Greek). He has travelled the world over, many times, and has represented clients, in his thirty five year career, such as the United States Government and the Federation of Russia.

He has been a prosecutor three times in his 35 year career. He has held positions such as Assistant Attorney General, United States Speaker, and Assistant District Attorney, Chief Wing JAG, U. S. Air Force Auxiliary, and Supreme Court Law Clerk.

For most of his career in civil law, John was a successful international lawyer, practicing in many nations around the world.

Now Available

How to Avoid False Accusations of Rape

Self Defense in the Feminist State

John Davis BA JD LLM

End Notes

www.ingramcontent.com/pod-product-compliance
Lightning Source LLC
Chambersburg PA
CBHW070229210526
45168CB00019B/274